A Peace At A Time

E.G. STANHOPE

WESTBOW
PRESS®
A DIVISION OF THOMAS NELSON
& ZONDERVAN

This book is a work of non-fiction. Unless otherwise noted, the author
and the publisher make no explicit guarantees as to the accuracy of
the information contained in this book and in some cases, names of
people and places have been altered to protect their privacy.

WestBow Press books may be ordered through booksellers or by contacting:

WestBow Press
A Division of Thomas Nelson & Zondervan
1663 Liberty Drive
Bloomington, IN 47403
www.westbowpress.com
844-714-3454

ISBN: 978-1-6642-6961-3 (sc)
ISBN: 978-1-6642-6960-6 (e)

Print information available on the last page.

WestBow Press rev. date: 7/27/2022

I LOVINGLY DEDICATE THIS BOOK TO: my daughter and my grandsons who have all blessed me from their birth. They have lived the story and still love me. "May you come to better understand God, who created you, and the woman who wrote this book. May you discover God's purpose for your lives through a personal relationship with Jesus Christ. I love you more than you will ever know."

CONTENTS

ACKNOWLEDGEMENTS

MY EVERLASTING PRAISE AND LOVE TO GOD: for his patience through my self-centered past, for never giving up on me, for giving me my new nature and forgiving all that I had been. For the guidance I receive through Jesus Christ and the Holy Spirit in my daily life, and for the peaceful security of knowing I have eternal life with a loving God.

I GRATEFULLY THANK: my daughter, grandsons, mother, sisters, and nephews who gave their support, love and blessing to the content and spirit of the book. And to my father, who never knew about the book, but would have approved.

MY DEEP APPRECIATION: To friends and family who were trusted to read the early drafts of this book. They may not have always understood me or agreed with me, but were constant in their support and encouragement. I am privileged to be included in their lives.

THANK YOU to the editor: of my work. His professional skills, suggestions and encouragement were invaluable to me as a first time author.

THANK YOU to my longtime friend: who is a part of my story. She is my age but light years ahead of me technically. She has patiently guided, led, and dragged me through the process of all the mechanical aspects of writing, without her help this book would still be suited up and sitting on the launch pad.

INTRODUCTION

The following testimony reveals my "Near God" experiences and my solid "Now God," experiences which give me an unshakable, secure freedom in a loving relationship with God.

Where have I been all my life? How had life's meandering path brought me to this place a small, dreary town of four hundred people, at the foot of a mountain range in Southern Wyoming? Not enough people here to fill a small apartment complex in the city where I had lived for fifteen years. Not the "Life in the West" of youthful vision. My heart whispered, "When you spend your life following other people's expectations your own misguided judgment, lust, and ego, buffeted and tossed like a rudderless boat, you get lost." In my world, people were constantly thwarting God's plan, believing all the while that this was life, each one struggling to gain control and direction in their lives.

The "cowboy" of my dreams had cut a deep hole in my heart, and although we were still married, he was not in my life. I had placed him on an ice floe and pushed him out to sea. His departure became a stimulus for my seeking and then finding life God's way.

I settled into my lodge pole pine chair, cuddling in the green and burgundy afghan Mother had crocheted for me. I had a pencil and legal pad in hand, intending to construct the outline of a book. A book was emerging in my head, not the great historical novel of youthful dreams, but the history of my life and rebirth into a life in Christ.

I could not write anything that night; instead I spent time in prayer, asking God how to witness about my life in Christ. I was too new to Christianity and believing and I could not reference anything I said, felt, or experienced using scripture, in--depth interpretation, or definite knowledge of the Bible. I was just beginning to read the Bible. Yet I had this powerful urge to tell of the peace on the other side of the chasm that separates us from God.

The answer to my prayer was not long in coming. A few nights later, I was awakened at one a.m. with energy and purpose, my head exploding with ideas. I sat down at the computer and began to outline chapters. I wrote a foreword and began the first chapter. The words came almost faster than I could type. Three hours later, exhausted, I stumbled back to bed.

In the morning, approaching the computer with coffee in hand, I hesitantly called up the nights work, reading words I knew were written with a divine direction. Convinced my testimony had value, I knew God would give me the confidence and skill to finish the story. Even though I was a new Christian, I knew my entry level testimony would speak to others. God could work through me if I was willing to make myself available to simultaneously do the work of growing in Christ, exposing my life honestly, and learning while writing.

In June 2002, I had begun to write a book with the working title *I Am My Own White Knight*. I began reading this earlier effort in a surreal state of mind, as if reading someone else's work. I was stunned by the sardonic, cynical words and thoughts "she" had written and was saddened to the point of tears. She struggled to move everything forward perfectly in her own world without the benefit of two-thirds of the Holy Trinity. That writer was constantly discontented, angry, frustrated and in plan-and-control mode. Yet she was not without value: I could use the old me to convey to a potential audience how far God had brought me at almost warp speed.

My heart and my body bear a silent testimony to the scars many of us carry; the loss of a child, miscarriage, divorce, automobile accidents, cancer, failed projects, betrayal, unholy alliances and most important, the self-inflicted pain of ego-driven decisions. It is a daily amazement to me I spent over forty years in a self-made wilderness because I refused, missed or ignored the message of salvation at every opportunity. I did not understand who Jesus was and did not see that he, the Holy Spirit, and the word of God were the missing pieces in my life.

Now I have the pieces, and I will never let them go. I can look back on my life, with all its painful effort, and thank God for putting me back into the fire all those times until I learned to praise him for the opportunity of trial. I now have the life that is available only through God's sacrificial gift to his children, Jesus Christ, the promised messiah. My prayer is God will speak to you through my testimony and send you seeking your own salvation.

AUTHOR'S MISSION AND PURPOSE

Having searched the file drawers for the notes written by that frustrated old self, I sat staring at the content of the aborted book, *I Am My Own White Knight.* The night rain in the valley was falling in a steady Seattle kind of mist, and the fragrance of wet sage blended with the aroma of fresh-brewed coffee. I poured a cup and settled back into my chair to review that first attempt to write a book. I intended to write about how heavy the burden of "Lord Over All" is, for those of us who believe we are chosen to carry it. I had looked down on born-again Christians as phonies who would not take responsibility for their lives. I denied anyone could really know they had an eternal relationship with God, without working for it. Each time God was calling me to right relationship my ego and pride said no to the invitation.

I meant *White Knight* to be penned in bile, a shining example of my sarcasm, to prove to a literary audience that a tough and proactive stance must be taken at every turn in order to make life work. I would explain how we are forced to spend precious energy designing our own moral code to align with each decision that comes across our desks. Later I learned it takes all one's pride, arrogance, ego, anger, and energy spent minute by minute to justify our ego driven actions to try to make life work. I was defined and accepted by my perceived strength, take-charge attitude, and ability to handle crisis, anyone's crisis. I lived my life as the combined holographic perception of other people. I guarded who I deeply desired to be by pushing my dreams into the dark corner where I could visit them. I told myself that someday when I had met all the needs around me I would have time for my dreams. By setting them on a shelf, I could also avoid ridicule, vulnerability, and loss of control, keeping my persona of strength. I believed my purpose in life was to solve every problem brought to me and to be the trauma center for those who laid their brokenness at my feet, saying "What would you do?" I honestly thought I had to answer.

I had never read another person's testimony. What made me think I could write mine or write anything to reach others? God was moving in a mighty way in my life, clearly saying, "I gave you a gift of communication and called you to witness for me. Your gift was not intended for your destructive attempt to control your existence, or to spew your poison into the minds of others." God had reached me in his perfect timing, as I was about to use my gift to, once again, run amuck in the world. He promised to be with me as I stepped out to talk about my transforming experience. It was six a.m. when I walked out onto the deck for a few minutes of morning air and sounds and then back to bed hoping to reclaim a few of the missing hours of sleep.

My acceptance of Jesus as the Lord of my life on September 27, 2003 and the birth of my real connection to God were meteoric events. God picked me up and shook me so powerfully and taught me so rapidly who he was, and what he wanted from me that it still staggers me. At the writing of this piece of the book, it is five years since I found the only one to trust without question to be there for me. The peace, unfailing love and completeness are the gifts of relationship that can never be equaled in any human experience. I am writing this book because God is calling me to do so. I do not consider myself an instantaneous theologian. I write under God's direction, believing my testimony will ignite a spark in one or more hearts to claim relationship with Jesus Christ and secure their own eternal future with God.

Once we know Christ, we must share our testimony; in hope of reaching others who are ready to lay down the burden of self-direction who wrongly believe being a good person and doing good works are all one needs to enter the kingdom of Heaven. Those who believe they have an intellectual and therefore, by their own definition, superior understanding of God and his inspired word; those with no understanding of the Holy Trinity or knowledge of right relationship with God through Jesus Christ; those who know the Bible must be important but cannot understand or read it and are frustrated with their inability to access the information; those who think they must have a human leader standing between them and God; and those who consider Jesus just a good teacher of moral principle who died for his self-appointed cause.

I was there, with all those beliefs and more at varying points in my life, and without God's merciful forgiveness at the moment of clarity, I would have missed my gift of salvation. Not only did he forgive me and say "This moment is the real beginning of your life", but he willingly took my pride, arrogance, and all my transgressions, pain, and misguided thoughts and deeds away forever. I was set free of all that baggage, and it was freeing and frightening just like a physical birth, when you are ripped from the dark into light and air, cleaned up, wrapped in a blanket, and delivered to the one who loves and nurtures you and helps you grow.

For those of us who have said, "If I could just start over, be given a second chance", we are looking for relationship with the living Jesus Christ. We are looking for the true and only path to God. We want to be renewed in spirit, to have that second chance, but we want it on *our* terms. So we search one philosophy after another looking for the one that will give our interpretation of what God offers but with us structuring the deal.

A personal relationship with Jesus Christ with all its wondrous blessings and secured future is ours for the asking, but on God's terms. God created us, and we are his. When we humbly surrender ourselves to have a relationship with him, it can only be on his terms: he owns the deal. True Christianity requires complete surrender. There are many false teachers and idols ready to serve up their style of "path" to God, but there is only one God and one way to eternal life. God is the Father who truly knows what is best for his children. We cannot make a better plan for our lives than God has planned for us. There is even a plan for those of us who have wandered around in the wilderness of pride until we are due for an appointment with the Office of Social Security.

This book is not offered as a guide, a structure, or a series of tests you can take that will map out a conclusion about your life. Some chapters are a reflection on how close God was all through my life, how many times I missed the call to real relationship with God, until in his second-or-third-best but perfect timing the scales fell from my eyes. Other chapters recount my salvation experience and my new life in Christ.

This is not a book containing a compilation of case studies charting people's lives. That type of book tends to send us speed-reading with purposeful effort to find a box with a solution into which we can fit our own life. And when we don't find an exact match with ready solutions attached, we are disappointed and probably miss any real message the author had to offer.

I offer no tables, comparative charts, or statistics from which to define yourself. This is fallout from one life. I have no educational degrees with which to dazzle and amaze you. I am no self-proclaimed expert, religious leader or guru: just a woman who believed for fifty-nine years that building personal power and using it to control and direct people and circumstances would bring accomplishment and success. In the end, I finally discovered that personal power is a lie from hell. Thank you God, for not allowing me to be highly successful at anything I took on, because that would only have reinforced my "self-made person" theories. I cannot quote scripture or preach the paint off the walls, but with God's leading I can convey the message of how the power of transformation feels when it happens and as it grows. My hope is that these pages will connect the dots for some others who may suddenly see, hear and believe how critically important it is to choose and follow Christ.

Coming home to God through his precious Son, Jesus is not an event with a beginning and end. It is not something we do in an emotional moment swept along with crowds of people trying to suddenly assuage a guilty past. It is not a stopping point but a deeply personal passage through an invisible framework with no turning back and no hesitation. It is personal *commitment* and *surrender* on a scale that permanently teaches us what those words mean. You will not want to go back; instead, you will change so drastically from the inside out it will both terrify you and make you completely secure. When we slip up or backslide and scramble in fear of defeat to get back on track we know we are safe because we have God's promise that he will never forsake or leave us.

Our first priority becomes our relationship with our Father, his Son and the Holy Spirit who comes to live in us and become the compass in our lives. It is relationship we need, intimate, personal, one on one, lost in love, right relationship with the one who knows everything about us and loves us in spite of ourselves. To surrender our lives to God through Jesus Christ causes us to walk past what pathetic little we have managed to scrape into a pile and call our accomplishments and possessions, to step into a world of a continuing supply of all our needs (not necessarily wants) to fulfill God's plan for our lives. A life committed to Christ, gives us incredible freedom to become the persons we were meant to be, and in our deepest recesses, the persons we always wanted to be.

We now have real "Choice", choice between living in the truth of intelligent sovereign design or dying by swimming in the juice of our limited intelligence. If we want to "use our own brains", we must use them and our hearts to connect to the real power source, the God who created us, in a deep personal relationship through his son Jesus Christ. It does not matter what man made "church structure" you now belong to, you are still in need of personal relationship with God through Christ, as God defined it in his word. Christ defined the "Church" as, who so ever will follow me. Christians are believers in Christ as savior and Lord of their lives, who live by God's word.

The energy it takes to constantly be in charge of designing, guarding and maintaining the ever changing schematic of our own lives, will leave us exhausted, bitter, and frustrated with ourselves and others. This secular world and our own human nature are designed to destroy us. And until we understand, and in humble surrender seek the gift of salvation by asking forgiveness and turning to Christ, we will struggle in pain, fear, frustration, bitterness and self-centeredness, until the end of our physical lives when we are judged by God, only then realize to what end our stubborn, baseless rebellion against our creator has brought us. It will then be too late to receive his Grace and mercy.

CHAPTER ONE

BORN ON THE EDGE
OF WILDERNESS

Since my entrance into this world, I have been one of the many people who never have enough financial security to fully relax and enjoy life, but never have so little they qualify for agency support. Since my birth, every self-directed move has been a struggle. Not the kind of struggle or crisis that makes headlines and hooks the heart of the nation, or produces a huge Save This Person Fund with unlimited financial resources upon which to draw. Not the kind of struggle that tests your will and mine to keep going, because the carrot is still visible out there ahead of you, even though in the right light it appears to be rotting. This is the kind of struggle only a human being relying on self can create.

The day my mother delivered me they quarantined the hospital due to a flu outbreak; a portent which should have been seriously considered in my rearing. My father and eight-year old sister kept a constant stream of daily postcards coming but no visits. Finally my mother and I were allowed to go home. Like the cue ball in the break of a game of billiards, I entered the well ordered world of my quiet conservative parents and grandparents, all four of whom had doted on and hovered over my well-behaved sister for eight years. Eighteen months later I was joined by my own baby sister and between the two of us we changed the family dynamics by introducing chaos.

I grew up as an overweight child in a time when such a transgression against humanity would have got you the pillory, if it had still been allowed by law. I now am reasonably invisible as I move among a major percentage of the population. I was simply ahead of my time. The society around me clearly made my "transgression" a matter of my choice and control; therefore my fault. Fifty years passed before the medical profession discovered I had a thyroid problem.

I was the child with the sprained ankle from playing baseball, the broken finger from falling into bed, the jack-knife injury incurred while climbing a tree, the rat bite, the tonsillectomy at seventeen. I struggled through school never, according to the teachers and counselors, achieving my potential. I saw the world from a different mountaintop, which was not a popular concept in the 1950s. That movement hove into view in the early sixties. By then I was well on my forced march to a Midwest conservative position in life. I never could find my place, thinking all the time I had been born either twenty minutes too soon or too late. Otherwise, my entry into the stream of life would have taken place at the smoothly flowing section.

I had friends, but unlike them, I wasn't particularly interested in the activities that were age appropriate. I considered the teen years a dead zone in which one waited for the day of adult acceptance. I much preferred the company of adults and had more comfortable conversations with the parents of my peers than I did with my friends. My core dream was to paint brilliant work that would illustrate the books I wanted to write.

My first family vacation was a trip to Colorado at age seven. That was when I realized that living in the West would be the third part of my dream. Making it through the year to summer vacation each year was like slogging through wet concrete to reach the departure day that would take me to the mountains. In my heart, from that early age, I knew I would live out all my deepest desires under Western skies. We made a trip every year, and my heart ached when we had to turn the car around and head back east, watching out the rear window until the last range of mountains melted into the western horizon. This ache and longing were connected to dreams I couldn't share with my parents. The dreams needed protection and nurturing that I sensed would be hindered by my family's opinions.

The neighborhood in which I was incubated and grew wings was a self-contained triangular section of the city bordered by two highways and a major road that connected us to the next town. The western point of the triangle was swamp and the creek. I spent glorious hours of exploration in the swamp. The southern triangle point exited to the shopping strip and the bowling alley. The northern point exited to the high schools. And the school bus took us out of the sacred walls of the neighborhood to grade schools scattered over the rest of the town. Church was four blocks from my home, as was the corner neighborhood store.

The corner store was the place to stop on the way home from school and the destination for summer excursions. The age of the store revealed itself in the rounded edges of the front steps, polished to a satin finish by thousands of feet sliding slowly over the edge as patrons passed through the door or spent time exchanging wisdom and gossip. The front door stood ajar shedding its dark green paint in the afternoon heat. Through that door were the icy cold treats of summer.

The candy jars lined the shelf like glass bubbles filled with a kaleidoscope of colors in the shape of sticks, balls, lips, beads, horns, cars and small candy children with their arms pressed to their sides. The cracked and cloudy glass in the display cases covered items for sale from another time: Souvenir cups and saucers, two satin pillows with gold fringe leaning against each other like two old maid aunts napping. A rack of greeting cards stood in the corner at a precarious slant crammed with cards and mismatched envelopes at various angles, looking tired from being fingered. There was a box of pink and green intricately woven straw finger pulls from China, and some small wooden pencil boxes painted with red and gold umbrellas on black bamboo.

A summer breeze drifted through the store's back door carrying with it the fragrance of peonies, mixed with the last of the lilacs and the acrid sweet spice of arborvitae, all blending with the odors of dust, produce, and the meat counter. The ceiling fan turned slowly, continually pointing out the gallery of poster ads on the wall, their yellowed edges curled like dry autumn leaves. Flies huddled under the fan motor circling without purpose in the eye of the storm.

As I approached the freezer, the vibration of the motor on the splintered plank flooring tickled the bottom of my feet. It stood like a square snowman guarding the back wall. I would open the freezer, and a brief gust of winter wind would pass over my face. Breaking the lime ice treat over the counter edge, I laid my nickel in the large hand that came over the counter somewhere near my nose. With one half of the summer treat in each hand I grabbed the handle grips of my bicycle, a maneuver only children can execute, and wobbled down the sidewalk with my frozen green signal lights dripping over my hands.

The store was taken from my world by a summer tragedy; the owner suffered a massive heart attack while at the meat counter and died. His wife sold the business, probably a good decision for her. However, my world seemed blown apart. We had neighbors, some of whom are still closely held friends. We were a neighborhood, functioning on a basis of in and out of each other's houses, borrow what you need, clean and patch up all the kids like family. The neighborhood made a safe, wonderful, and well-spun cocoon for my growing-up years. Moms were home when school was let out. Everyone watched out for the others, doors were left unlocked. I remember feeling sorry for the kids of the only two families to move away during my childhood.

Seasons were defined by unique and welcome characteristics. Summers in the mountains were my favorites, of course, fueling my spirit for school and the rest of the year. Crisp air and burning piles of leaves in early fall led to Thanksgiving. Winter ushered in the Christmas pageants, choirs, school programs. Santa visited all the houses in the neighborhood on the fire engine handing out gifts our parents had bought and wrapped for us the week before. Then spring festivals and Easter services, new Easter outfits, heralding the coming of summer vacation and freedom. All of it was marked with wonderful appropriate cutouts and signs made of construction and crepe paper, with bits of sticks, feathers, beads, and lace held together with generous amounts of library paste. Life was reasonably peaceful and secure for me growing up in a fifties sit-com existence, except for a massive confusion about Christianity.

My parents and grandparents were kind, loving people with standards and ethics for living that were admirable. We were loved and knew it. But the teaching of the Bible on a daily basis was not present in our home. Prayer was limited to grace before meals, and Sundays were for church.

From the age of nine, I wanted to know how to read and understand the Bible and was frustrated with my inability to understand what I thought everyone else knew.

When my much loved grandpa died suddenly of a massive coronary, diagnosed earlier in the day as the mumps, I ran to the car and sat crying in the backseat by myself. It was my first experience with death, and it was hard to get a hold of as I watched the adults around me dealing with the facts of his death. However, we did not gather together and read God's word. No one asked Jesus to comfort and give us strength.

We belonged to the Congregational church, in which I had been baptized; later I would be confirmed and married there, following in the footsteps of my older sister. In those times, generally, certain subjects were whispered about in front of children, subjects like religion (don't discuss it or bring it up) politics (don't discuss it or you will start an argument) sex (nice people don't discuss it) and finances (don't ask anyone about their money). I do not remember anything being taught about a personal relationship with Jesus. I decided I must be too young. Someday it would just happen to me; I would be washed over with knowledge and understanding.

All families are dysfunctional to one degree or another. Part of the dysfunction in my family was protection and sheltering from all of life's important lessons. Keeping life small, under control, safe a`la *Father Knows Best* was the goal. It's a little like being beaten to death with a Hallmark card, how can you raise a complaint? However, it does not prepare a woman to meet all that will be coming at her, but rather to be taken care of by the mythical white knight in shining armor, whose sole purpose in life is to adore her and let her do whatever she wants. Only after my first marriage dissolved did I understand how high the price of total dependency on another human.

When confirmation class began, I thought I would be taught how to read and understand the Bible. I was presented with a Bible on Confirmation Sunday. I do not remember ever being taught that the

Bible was the word of God, written by men whom God had chosen and inspired, that it was the operating manual for life, or that if I based my life on God's word and accepted his gift of salvation, he would guide me into the life he had planned for me. Instead I came away with the idea that the Bible was written by men who took it upon themselves to interpret the oral stories that were handed down through the generations. I knew nothing of a personal relationship with Jesus, nothing of becoming a new creature in Christ. My perception of God was distorted. I believed that God created everything, that he was the core of my being, and that he loved me, but that he expected me to use my brain to learn to handle my life and accomplish great things.

I saw God as the source to consult as I presented my plans for his approval. Jesus was his son, and if I was God's child too, I had equal access to God. I had no understanding of the Holy Trinity. I saw many examples of Christians who abused God's word, calling themselves Christians while breaking every one of the Ten Commandments. They sat on their pious posteriors waiting for God to solve all their problems, all the time adding to the pile. From those observations and my upbringing, I somehow concluded that God wanted workers and thinkers who would bring their plans to him for consultation, approval and blessing. The examples of Christianity in my youth included our Catholic friends being told in their church they were not to play with any non-Catholics because we were all heathens.

Personally, the teasing and barbed comments about my weight from a handful of adults every Sunday in church soured my view of the Christian family. Perhaps from that cruel exclusion, I seemed to be able to see through them and the hypocrisy of two-faced internal competition and politics as they pursued personal kingdoms or the wealth building business of church. I didn't want any part of it. At the other end of the spectrum, I did not want to be associated with people who howled up tent poles and handled snakes. Their spiritual offering didn't appeal to my longing for more knowledge of God and his word.

My first opportunity to encounter true Christianity came when I was fifteen and went with a friend to her church youth program. It featured a speaker who talked about the homeless people being served at the mission in the city. He wanted the youth group to come downtown and help serve food and hand out blankets and clothing. I can still remember the fire I felt at the prospect of being part of something so proactive and meaningful. This was the first missed call from God. Permission to go was denied. My parents told me this was not the type of program in which we participate and it was dangerous downtown at night.

I stopped taking communion in my late teens I did not want to be considered a Christian because, as presented, communion was meaningless. I wanted to have a direct relationship with God. I knew God was totally trustworthy, but the rest of it was confusing, hurtful, and lacking in substance. I resented the time my mother spent doing church related activities such as luncheons, sewing circle, mother-daughter banquets, potluck dinners and choir practice every Thursday night. I participated because I was expected to do so, but I resisted it all and became critical and sarcastic about almost all of what I saw as shallow.

I do not remember our church ever taking on social issues. We never grappled with anything that would seriously test the structure and tradition of a church that had been established in the pioneer years of the town. There were only white faces in our congregation. But I do remember our church's annual minstrel show where members of the adult congregation dressed in blackface and denigrated black Americans. It never seemed very godly to me.

I was never exposed to black Americans until I went to work after high school in a major department store in the city. The stock woman and I became work friends and I liked her very much. She took me under her wing and taught me about the store, and she did things to make the learning process easy for me. We had a similar sense of humor and had good giggles about some of the customers' behavior. Then one day a male friend of hers came in the department. The minute she spotted him she stopped talking in mid-sentence and walked away from me. Until the man left, she not only ignored me but looked at me with absolute disdain.

I was wounded by her attitude and did not know what I had done to make her dislike me so instantly. When he left, she disappeared into the stockroom and I did not see her until after the weekend. In my naiveté, it never occurred to me that prejudice came from both sides, or that the entire struggle in the south had anything to do with people who lived in my state. There were only four stations on the television, and I had no interest in the news which only aired for a half-hour at 6pm and again at 10.

The minister of our church, from the time I was two, was a powerful figure in my life. I did not know the questions to ask, though, and he gave himself so completely to others who were in crisis that I never felt my need to understand more about Christianity belonged in his busy schedule. He was a totally committed man who wore himself out in service and died in his fifties. He was my first pastor. I was fourteen when he left our church to take a pastorate in another state; I was traumatized, along with most of the congregation.

I had a dream when I was fifteen years old. In that dream I died and rose from my body and began to ascend in an upright position above the house then the trees. I saw the city fall away beneath my feet. As I rose higher I reached out to either side, and two hands closed around mine. One belonged to my father and the other to the minister of our church. As we ascended, the most powerful feeling came over me, as if I was leaving all earthly emotions and emerging into a new kind of love for these men. This emotional state was profound but peacefully detached, and yet powerfully comforting, I knew it was for eternity. From the moment I awoke I no longer feared death. I knew God had a plan for me. And if I had only known how critical it was to make Jesus the Lord of my life, I would not have had to wander in the desert for so many years.

The replacement minister was far removed from what I had known. Although I tried to keep an open mind, I became angry and physically gut wrenched in his presence. No one else in my world had a similar reaction which astonished me. I stopped going to church.

It was about this time, as I was searching for answers, that I was introduced to an alternative religious study. This new intellectual organization seemed to incorporate more self into its material, and I wanted support for my definition of relationship with God. I became a "light touch" student and read it for many years. It was something to hang my belief on, even though it often left me with questions concerning the veiled and illusive articles in the monthly publication. Often they contradicted each other and appeared to be inconclusive and insubstantial.

When I graduated from high school my parents bought me a ticket on the inaugural flight of the strata-cruiser airliner to my beloved West. My first flight was bringing me to work for family friends who owned a motel and store in the heart of the Rocky Mountains. I was to stay the summer and be picked up by my parents before the start of college in the fall. The experience turned out to be both glorious and devastating, a painful blow I carried with me for many years. The people I had trusted showed their dysfunction by trying to drive a wedge between me, my parents and my many new friends there, with jealous lies about me and my behavior during the summer.

They made my stay miserable, even though they had been the ones to call and ask me to work for them. This was because I was well liked by the town citizens and was invited to all the local parties which took place almost every night. Even though the store owners had been in town for eight years, they were not included. The summer home owners were there to relax and have fun. Because they brought most of their supplies with them, they did not purchase much from the store my employers owned. I found out through the summer, as I gained the town folks trust, the people I worked for were shunned for good reasons, mostly to do with financial dealings and an attitude of disdain toward the locals as distinct from tourists.

My employers painted a picture of me as an uncontrollable wild animal, who gave them nothing but trouble all summer. In reality, I had worked hard. I washed bedding and linens for the motel in a wringer washer and hung them out to dry. I worked at the store and was even instructed to dig trenches for the sewer line. I spent many evenings with the local families, singing around campfires at picnics and dances and enjoying good conversation.

I was furious when I heard the accusations. Worse I had no way to respond to them because my parents stayed for five days after they arrived to pick me up and never told me what my employer friends had said until after we left for home. When I asked why they did not give me a chance to confront them, my mother said she did not want a scene.

Anger and outrage were not acceptable in my family even if they were justified. As a child when I was mad about something or at someone my mother would say "Oh, you don't feel like that, that's not nice." Negative feelings of any kind were never validated and we were never taught how to resolve issues. Ignore it and it will go away.

Over this particular act of betrayal my stomach felt as if something wild was trying to scratch its way out. My face was hot, and I was choking back tears I wanted to confront my accusers and call them the liars they were but soon learned I was to be sacrificed to keep the friendship intact. I lost sleep and then woke up angry, hurt and plotting revenge every morning for almost a year.

A year after the incident the perpetrators of the lies and abuse came to town and called our home. My mother invited them over for dinner. Trapped, I was expected to be nice. I did not comply. If my own mother would offer me neither protection nor defense, then self-defense had to be the order of the day. By the time the guests left, they had a clear picture of my anger, and we never saw them again.

I had been violated, emotionally raped, and the assault on my character did not merit either protection or defense by my parents. A relationship with Jesus would have given me a place to put all the pain and move on. Because I did not have that relationship, I was nearly destroyed by the experience, until that opportunity presented itself, and I was able to verbally unload most of the bile that had churned inside me. Even though I gained some healing from standing up for myself, for years I carried the pain of the false accusations and emotional abuse I had suffered at their hands. The lack of outrage and defense from my mother left a large wound in my heart. It eventually scabbed over and stayed that way until my salvation through Jesus Christ. Later I was able to forgive her.

I came home from out West and prepared to go to college in the fall. At the same time, my former pastor suffered a severe heart attack and moved back to our area, blocks from the university in which I had enrolled. They were in need of someone to care for the family, because his wife had taken a teaching job. I moved in and used their second car so I could attend school and go home on the weekends. I did light housekeeping, fixed meals and looked after my much loved pastor and his wife and children. There were times I wanted to talk to him, but he was recovering from his heart attack and I did not want to apply any kind of pressure.

When Christmas rolled around a friend of the family, a former church member called them to say he would get the Christmas tree for them. I knew who he was but he was six years older and I did not really know him except by sight. I told him to come for dinner and we could take the kids with us to pick out the tree. We started dating and I quit school to get a job.

I wanted to move out west, but the choices in that day for most young women were nurse, teacher, secretary or wife. We were not encouraged to move away and follow our passion. The world was too frightening and hard, and girls needed to be "safely" married. To hear another call on your life was "fantasy talk" Conformity and conservative behavior would lead to approval and acceptance. Once again, my choices were made based on my limited knowledge and without a prayerful relationship with God through Jesus Christ.

My part in this rapidly developing but eventually disastrous relationship took a wild turn, almost a kink. I met someone else shortly after I met my future husband and was knocked off my pins by the intensity of my feelings for this new person. I reeled from emotions I had not even come close to experiencing in my short life. I had a hard time catching my breath from the moment we met. The feelings were mutual and hard to deal with. He scrambled my brain when I was close to him, and I ached when we were apart.

Eventually we were separated long enough for logic and reason to reenter my brain. The facts were simple: this breathtaking person was not free. I had just met my future husband, and although I felt nothing close to skyrockets when I was with him, at least I had control of my brain. I did not want to be so drawn to someone that I spun out of control, causing me to act like all the sappy women I had seen in the movies.

What in the world had happened to me? I was not a hopeless romantic by nature so what was I supposed to do with all these uncontrollable emotions? I could not define love. Was it the mind-bending, powerful, white hot passion that turned me into a blithering fool? Or was it the conventional, steady attention of the presumed white knight coming to take me off to "happily ever after"? In truth, I did not want either one on a permanent basis.

I was ignoring the burning desire I had for my life, which I did not recognize as God's plan. If I had been living a life centered on Christ I might have had the courage to turn away from all I had known to follow him. If I had known and loved Jesus Christ first above all, made him Lord of my life, and gone to him and the word of God when the emotional chaos was tearing me apart I believe I would have been given clarity on the difference between lust and love and received the strength to start down the path God wanted me to travel. I base that belief on how differently I have responded to challenges in the last several years of living and loving my new life and on discovering in the Bible the lessons and instructions which would have delivered me from the chaotic results of every single one of my decisions.

I decided that a liberal arts education was not my desire and that I wanted to go to art school in Colorado. I had begun researching how to accomplish it when my first husband asked me to marry him. He told me he realized I had talent and he would make sure that I had the art education I wanted. We could work together to accomplish it. Even though my heart wanted desperately to move west I gave in when he countered all my arguments. He treated me like a princess, answered my every wish, and presented all the gifts and care a woman could possibly want. Everyone in my world constantly repeated, "You will never find anyone who treats you as well as he does" I thought, *Does this mean I am so unworthy of being loved by someone that I better grab this opportunity before he opens his eyes? I am eighteen years old, and this is my only chance at happiness?* I had no one to talk to about such issues.

I remember thinking; *Women are just people who belong to men.* "You are your father's until he hands you over to another man" In the sixties you still heard single women referred to as spinsters and old maids people shook their heads and said, "Poor girl, she never found someone who wanted her" And if any woman stepped out of line or dared to express herself, her strength, or a hint of independent spirit, the verdict came down: "You know what her problem is she needs a man. She does not know how to keep her place"

The clear message was that marriage was the highest honor a man could bestow on you. Women's dreams had no substance; they were just fantasies, while men had valid dreams. The worst part of this pervasive attitude was that women shared it and joined in the judgment against each other. Women were taught that they were on their own when it came to competing for a man.

I was torn, thinking about my future life: frightened at the confinement of marriage, frightened about being pitied because I wasn't married, wanting to pack my things and head out west, wanting a totally different life than the one looming on the horizon. I felt a deep sadness, because my vision of life was not acceptable, had no value and I was at risk of separation from the people who were holding me too tightly. I became adept at faking and stuffing my feelings. I said yes to the proposal and started down a road that would take me far from God's calling.

CHAPTER TWO

MORE WILDERNESS: RIGHT THIS WAY

====

Here was the fork in the road of my forty-year journey to Jesus. If I had had a strong personal relationship with Christ, I would have had the courage to say no to the proposal. I would have moved in the direction God had planned for me. I was eleven days from the promise land. I caved into the pressure of parents who wanted me safe, to conventional behavior of the time. With no support for the calling I felt, I bought into the "safe" life. I now see how my fearful human nature overtook to confuse me, divert my attention, knock down my confidence, and bring me into line.

Wedding plans began. We were married February 1964, in the church we had both attended since childhood, by the minister we both loved. It was a beautiful wedding with all the "must be done" and appropriate details. Even the maintenance man remarked how he had never witnessed a happier wedding.

My husband planned a wonderful honeymoon, a trip through the West in a newly purchased Thunderbird. It was a month of romance, glamour, and lavish good fun. When we came home we moved into a cozy little rental house, surrounded by all the new possessions. That was the end of the promised land of "happily ever after". The person I had married disappeared like a character at the end of a film.

One day he came home in a four-door Plymouth sedan. He had traded in the Thunderbird without a word to me. Then the bills started piling up on the desk. I, who had never even had a checking account, asked when he planned to pay them. He answered, "I will do it, they can just wait". Since second notices were appearing, I began to panic. After all, when you are raised to be taken care of, if you are married, this is not supposed to be an issue for you to handle. Paying bills, was, as far as I knew, the husband's job.

Fear drove me to sit down with the stack and begin the arduous task of understanding bills. I remember clearly how nervous I was writing the first check I had ever written. Bill paying became my job, or it was not going to happen. I fell into the rest of my "duties" and followed in the path of my older sister, friends, and neighbors which was a routine of ironing and watching soap operas, grocery shopping and planning meals, falling in line with all the seasonal ceremonies and calendar events that mark off one's life. Conform, because there is nothing else.

We had been renting the house for four months when the landlord decided to sell. I wanted to buy it. At the same time, my husband's parents decided to sell their house and my husband wanted to buy that one. I gave in to his apparent need to finally have some decisive control over his childhood home. Thus began ten years of a roller-coaster ride: moving from house to larger house, remodeling, selling, and repeating the process, monumental projects which did not include art school or any piece of my dream. My choices were all wrong because they were not based on God's plan for my life. If I had had a strong relationship with Jesus Christ, a daily prayer life, and the word of God as my go-to move, I would have had the guidance system for my choices.

Four months after returning from our honeymoon, we began remodeling our first home. I had been taking birth control pills since January. I was a mess emotionally. I had gained weight and had developed an edema problem from the pills. The weight gain continued and I eventually wound up in the hospital. This was the first major "for better or worse" event in our marriage. It produced emotional distance rather than support from my husband.

The doctor took twenty-four pounds of fluid from my body overnight. He sent me home after a few days with medication that caused me to sit in a chair and drool for most of the day. I stopped taking the pills after three days. I never went back to see him. I stopped the birth control pills and became pregnant shortly after. We were thrilled. I love children, and was very excited about being a mother.

Early in my pregnancy I was plagued with irrational fears. Pictures of horrible things happening under very ordinary circumstances during my day would flash into my head. I would freeze in fear. I opened the basement door to take a load of laundry downstairs. I looked down at the bottom of the stairs. I pictured a figure holding a spear. I saw myself tripping and falling through the air and landing on the tip, driving the spear through my belly. I was shaking so hard I could not take a step and simply closed the door. I had many shocking, mental snapshots overtake me in the eight months I carried my son. They were combined with a constant, pervasive dread.

We were surrounded by family and friends, having both grown up in the same town. Yet no one had planned a shower. It was January, and we had not bought one thing for the baby who was due the first of March. My husband had contacted a friend who owned a damaged freight company. He asked him to be on the lookout for a crib, but that was all we had done.

One day in the last week of January, I developed a low backache. Chills, blue legs and low pelvic pain followed. I called the doctor's office. My amateur thespian doctor was busy starring in a play. His partner, whom I had never seen, told me to come to the hospital. He, in his arrogant wisdom gave me an enema and then left the hospital before he knew the results. Since I had not eaten for two days, I did not see how that could solve the problem. I went back home and could not sit because of the pelvic pressure. I paced the floor until I was exhausted enough to sleep.

At one in the morning, I got up to go to the bathroom, the pressure in my abdomen was intense and soon there was blood on the white tile walls and floor. My husband, instead of calling an ambulance, drove me to the hospital. I lay in a hospital room from 2 am until noon the next day. When my doctor had sufficiently recovered from his debut in amateur theater and the after-hours party, he finally took the time to make rounds. He took one look at me and had me in surgery within fifteen minutes. I had had numerous shots of painkillers and lost five and one half pints of blood waiting for him.

The baby's head had dropped three days before and blocked the opening. I had been bleeding internally until the pressure became so great it had blown. The staff and my doctor's brilliant partner had told me all night they could hear the baby's heartbeat. They had lied. He was dead, and I was very close to joining him. I never passed out. I knew I was not going to die. I knew God was there. The brilliant partner was sued eight months later for leaving an eight-inch forceps in a woman, an action which led to gangrene and removal of a section of her bowel. These were the people who held our lives in their hands.

The doctors did not have an answer as to why I was still alive. After an emergency cesarean, which was not carefully done because they did not expect me to live, they made a cruel decision to put me in a room across from the nursery. The torture of listening to precious newborns crying twenty-four hours a day was more than I could take. I was alone in my room and started to cry. I did not ring for anyone or ask for any help. I just cried from pain, loss, and fear. I did not know where my baby was, what had happened to his body. I was exhausted from surgery and loss of blood.

The charge nurse came in and stood at the end of my bed. She proceeded in a loud and irritated voice to tell me to stop acting like a spoiled child. I was not, in her words, "the first woman to lose a child and would not be the last". I was so shocked I could not speak. She left as quickly as she had launched her attack. When my husband came in I told him what happened. He left the room. I don't know what he did or who he spoke to, but I never saw her anywhere in the hospital for the ten days I was there.

I went home with empty arms. The phone call about the crib came a month after I had arrived home without my son. I was watching the new color TV my husband had bought as a replacement for our loss. What little ground I had gained fighting depression was lost as I stood holding the phone, solitary, barely able to say we would not need a crib.

My husband and I never discussed our son or our feelings about this major loss. He appeared to consider it a slight bump in the road. I just buried all my feelings. The messages were clear that this was another issue not to be talked about. I spiraled into depression heading for oblivion. I fought on my own every day to find air and light. Comments from people, many of whom considered themselves Christians were intended to be comforting. Strangely, they never included Jesus Christ in their words. They said, "You are young, you can have more." This was the unkindest remark of all, because it devalued the individual life of the child.

My baby was dead. I never said good-bye. He never had a funeral or a burial. I do not know to this day how the medical community disposed of him. I was angry, scared, bitter, and wounded to my depths. I believed it was something I either had or had not done that caused this tragedy. I found no human comfort. My definition of God did not include personal comforting. Once again I just ran over the event with daily life. I hoped that time would take the pain away. I spent endless years trying to suppress it.

One morning during my sixth month of pregnancy I had been rushing to get to a doctor appointment. I entered through the side door instead of the main door of the garage. I opened my car door and put my purse in the car, meaning to then open the garage door. Instead, I got in and backed up. I hit the garage door with enough force to jam the steering wheel of my VW bug into my belly. I could not forgive myself for being so brain fogged. I was convinced for years that my actions contributed to his death.

I was twenty-two years old and experiencing a trauma for which I had no preparation. I had never known of anyone losing a baby before birth. The stories began to surface as family and friends revealed similar pain in their own lives. I felt betrayed; why had no one told me this was a possibility? The doctors never gave me any information on how it had happened. I needed to know more.

I now know the strength I would have had in Christ to deal with that trauma. How comforting it would have been to know then that my baby was with God. Jesus would have been there for all of us, if we had been a truly Christian couple. There was no one who stepped forward to introduce either of us to Jesus Christ. Instead, I again believed God wanted me to make myself strong, "get back to work, put this behind me". The lack of communication or intimacy between my husband and me over our son's death was the beginning of our eventual divorce.

It is so important for Christians to take opportunities to talk about what Jesus has done for them. We never know who might be helped by our testimony and conviction. All those feelings and pain were just stuffed inside my body unresolved. I began to stuff myself with food to insulate and medicate against the pain. Four months later I was again pregnant. My body was so out of whack, and I was still suffering depression and exhaustion from the remodeling of the house and life in general, that I miscarried in the fourth month, another ordeal, fraught with depression, panic attacks, and more pain.

My position on abortion at that point in my life was very self-centered. It was not something I could ever do. I considered it a personal decision for each woman to make. I was vocal about not understanding how anyone could decide to take an unborn life. But it was their choice. It certainly did not require violent demonstrations. Why would such a personal issue require public involvement?

Here again, my position was based on my level of emotional security. I was loved as a child and had been taught to love children and value life. My position followed my perception that God expected us to make rational decisions based on our individual needs. He left these decisions to us. I had no knowledge of all the human scenarios being played out in the world, all the women making decisions using their uniquely battered and broken experience as the basis for their choices. I never even thought about desperation, panic, abuse, rape, mentally challenged women, women in prisons, women suffering depression and despair.

I felt no connection with all women. I was not that interested in people in general. I felt set apart—even worse, I felt set above most people. I had no social conscience, no worldview, and no real compassion for people who did not use "common sense." These seeds grew in me to produce arrogance and pride, an absolute conviction that I really knew the best way for people around me to live their lives. I was not cruel or mean to anyone … more like a benevolent dictator. I developed a style of sarcasm and humor compatible with my egocentric attitude. A protective shield, it seemed to work to my advantage as I moved through life.

I changed doctors and began going to the son of the doctor who delivered me. He was very kind and understanding. He suggested I give my body a rest for at least a year before starting a family. We followed the plan.

One year and eleven months later, by cesarean section, I gave birth to a beautiful, healthy baby daughter. She was and is such a miracle in my life. I felt so blessed, so grateful to God for the gift of a healthy child. I marveled at everything she did and adored her. It was difficult for me to be away from her for even an hour. I am privileged to be her mother. The very best of both of us was born in her. The world is better because she is here.

I never gave up on my dream to live out west. It brewed constantly in the back of my brain. Life went on, in the hectic pattern of new parents. We were now living in a newer larger house located in the neighborhood of my youth. With the help of all the women who watched me grow up, I was learning to be a well-organized, creative homemaker and mother. On the surface, we looked like a happy couple. There were many times of surface fun, friends, and celebrations. It was just day to day keeping it going, hoping for things to improve.

The turmoil of my emotions never left me. I just carried on. The world does not stop and give us time to reflect, adjust, or confront when we are only of the world. When we are controlled and driven by the circumstances of life, we respond the way we are expected to respond. We put our real selves on hold or in storage.

To avoid the pain of loneliness, I began to think more about the other fork in the road. I considered the consequences and the blessings of my decision to take this one. I longed for the mountains, the West, and my "cowboy's" love. Those intense feelings crowded my thoughts and distanced me from my reality. The memory of the man I had met before I married never left me. I was able to set him on a shelf and dust him off on occasion. But the unhappier I became in real time, the more I thought about him. I was splitting apart internally. I was Mid-west normal on the outside, and screaming in terror on the inside. I felt so trapped, so panicked, I would sometimes lose my breath.

This was the nineteen sixties. Divorce was not something normal people did. I only knew one person who was divorced. She had an acceptable reason: her husband had cheated on her. I was twenty-five years old and wanting a divorce for reasons difficult to express. I had a baby to raise and no way to make a living; an unthinkable situation. I was too naïve, trained to be scared to death of "what people would think." Image was everything in that era. There was not much help for a woman who attempted to step out on her own.

My husband was famous for his ability to work hard at everything he tackled. Everyone praised him for his accomplishments. No project was too large to take on. He was thought of as a wonderful husband and father by friends and family. No one knew, and I believed no one could have understood why I was so miserable. I knew I was destined to live in the West. I could never have predicted the way it would happen.

CHAPTER THREE

WILDERNESS: THE EARLY YEARS

The day came when my husband was offered a position out west. Many years later I learned the position was engineered by his boss, our former pastor, who could not deal with my husband's aggressive, pressuring nature.

Isolation from all family and friends brought out his true character. He no longer had to perform as the ideal husband and father. We celebrated Easter a month after we moved into our new home. My husband announced he was going flying with one of the board members from work on Sunday. He left me and my daughter alone on a holiday in a strange community.

It was then I realized I was no more than an acquisition on my husband's to-do list for life. Grow up, graduate, get a job, work hard, move up, and get married. He apparently thought that once you install a wife in a house and have a child, home will spin successfully with very little attention. As long as I performed my duties, kept things running relatively smoothly, and did not expect anything in a personal or intimate way, we functioned mechanically without discord.

The next three years were filled with exploring our new world of mountains and deserts. We made new friends, entertained out-of-town guests, and adjusted to life on our own. We lived in a beautiful older neighborhood with charming homes and older families. The two homes directly across the street were occupied by couples whose children were grown and almost gone. They became surrogate grandparents and close friends. Their friendship helped fill some of the empty places in my heart.

Our marriage continued to deteriorate. The thought of divorce was overwhelming. Then debilitating fear overtook me when I considered living out my life married and alone. We were living a believable lie, and it was taking its toll on me physically and emotionally.

To add to the pressure my husband met a professional convicted con artist. He arrived in town freshly released from a prison in the Midwest. He moved in on our community with a wife and three children. He had no job but all the skills from his previous career intact. He talked his way into a job with the owner/editor of the only opposing newspaper to the major newspaper in town. The con managed to destroy the paper and the owner. The owner was a very strong, intelligent man who fearlessly rooted out the truth of the political climate. He succumbed to the con's manipulation, lost his business, and was forced to move out of town.

My husband was no match for the con. This man had racked up over three hundred years of time. He managed to convince the state he had changed. He asked for a chance to go back to his family and raise his children. This happened during a time when prisons were housecleaning and setting "lesser offenders" free on the world. It was not long before he convinced my husband to begin the process of mortgaging our home. He suggested combining the proceeds with our cash and running up our credit cards to go into business with him. We were about to lose everything.

My stomach clutched every time this "magician" was present in a room. This time I listened to my rigid diaphragm. The fear of losing our home and the memory of what had happened to the newspaper owner gave me the courage to stand against them. They needed my signature. I refused to sign any paperwork. End of problem. The con moved on to fresh fields ready for picking.

My husband was not happy with me, but he recovered. We had just escaped the very personification of evil. I thanked God for his deliverance. However, I was very proud of myself for recognizing what was happening and standing up to them. I was so full of myself that I took most of the credit for turning the tables. I know now who really pulled us out of the fire.

Life rolled on. I struggled to find a calm and intellectual end to our marriage. I tried to talk to a husband who did not want to discuss the matter. His solution was to buy another house and begin remodeling it. He thought if he kept me busy, my need to resolve issues would disappear. I had left the marriage years earlier—or, as I now reflected, had never been in it. I could not understand why we could not just recognize its demise and end it amicably. He did not love me that was clear. He could be free to find someone else to fill the wife position.

My health deteriorated from the internal stress of all that had happened. I prayed every day for a way out. I was in need of support. I decided to try attending a church. I found a Congregational church only a few blocks from our house. The first Sunday we attended services, the minister came down the steps from his office, his robe blowing in the breeze, to greet us. The moment he took my hand I knew he would be my way out.

I know now that message was not from God, even though I credited him with it. Within the same time frame, we became good friends with my husband's secretary and her husband. She invited us to her home to meet her husband and have dinner with them. They were "born-again" Christians and attended the Baptist church. She began to gently encourage me to come to church with her before I made a commitment to the church we were attending. I turned away from God's invitation to come closer, just when I needed all that God was offering.

Over the course of time she pressed a little harder on each encounter. I argued with her, criticized her position, and finally had to ask her to stop trying to brainwash me. Our friendship stayed healthy and strong in spite of her effort to share the gift with me. And again, I turned in the wrong direction. Here was God trying to give me the understanding I had been asking for all my life. I, in my pride, rejected it.

We did join the Congregational church. A short time later, I called to make an appointment with the pastor. I was finally ready to talk about my marriage and ask for his help. Over many months of agonizing decisions and conversations, he was my lifeline. He and his wife became my good friends. I leaned heavily on him. As I look back from the perspective of my new life, I was putting my faith in him instead of God. He took on the responsibility of caring for me instead of directing me to develop a personal relationship with Christ.

He was a wonderful person. But, though I was grateful for his incredible support and help, I know now we were both floundering. The word of God was not brought to bear on the problem even one time. Jesus Christ was not even mentioned in any of our conversations. His was an intellectual approach. It was based in human emotions and human solutions. He was a major part of a huge turning point in my life. Once more I had chosen the comfort zone. With my counselor's help, I took on a two-year struggle of trying to "figure out" what to do, how to proceed with my life. Then one day I looked in the mirror and said, "This is it, no more, it is over." No more trying to plan this divorce. I filed the papers and jumped into the fray with both feet.

The divorce was finalized. Then the battle to receive alimony and child support on time, ensued. Every month I struggled to pay bills and get myself into a position to find work. I had had the audacity to obtain a divorce in the middle of a culture and time that considered women to be newly rebellious chattel. I was punished by a male-dominated society and court for daring to file for divorce.

We had been married just over ten years. I had not worked outside the home for all that time. My ex-husband did everything in his power to wreak havoc and injury in our lives. He was merciless in his emotional battering and selfish actions concerning his daughter. He was not one to lose at anything, even if he did not want it. I lived in fear of him taking my daughter by proving to a court that I could not provide for her.

It was during this time my husband's now former secretary made another attempt to lead me to Christ. She and her son invited me over for the evening. They began in earnest to tell me how much I needed Christ in my life. They worked on me for over four hours, gently but firmly. I was polite but repulsed by some of the words and phrases. "Washed in the blood of the Lamb" particularly made me sick. They told me I was not going to heaven. There was only one way, and I was not "on the path." I questioned why a loving God would punish and reject "his children." Now I understand it is because his children are disobedient and reject his sacrifice, his love and mercy. We refuse to humble ourselves before him and ask forgiveness. God has no choice but to turn us over to ourselves. And though it grieves him, he is perfect in his love and in his justice. God does not condemn us. We condemn and punish ourselves.

My friend said, "God is so clearly calling you into relationship. As a Christian I am called to do everything I can to bring you to your acceptance of salvation." I felt everything imaginable but peace, love, and joy at the prospect of joining the world of Christianity. *Fanaticism, cult, mindless robots, intellectual midgets,* these were the words that crowded my mind. I asked myself, "How could I love this friend so much? We are so far apart in our spiritual life—she is so committed to such a lemming-like interpretation of God."

All my life I had been asking God for his help, and each time he sent it, I rejected it. I never saw the obvious invitation as coming from God through his chosen messengers.

I kept swimming furiously against the current, constantly exhausted in my effort to conquer all the enemies and claim the victory alone. I was so sure of what God wanted of me—so sure I just had to work harder or smarter, and I could achieve perfection—when all I needed was walking right beside me. God was waiting for me to reach out and give my life with all its baggage back to him.

I was closer than I had ever been to being led to Christ. I stood up and asked them to please let me leave in peace. I cried all the way home. My life was coming apart. Now I had been told that God would turn from me. He would condemn me to hell if I did not believe what the Baptists believed. It frightened me to see how zealous and relentless they were in their pursuit of my soul. I loved my friend, so we just never talked about the subject again. She said she knew that someday I would accept Christ. I was so clearly his child. She just hoped she could live long enough to know me as a Christian. She didn't, but now I know I will see her again.

We sold our house. I moved into a rental house across the alley. My daughter had to suffer the epicenter as well as the aftershocks of divorce. The people who bought our house became my friends. Now their children owned my daughter's tree house and playroom. We had to sell the dollhouse we had made for her, along with some of her other things. She had to get used to all her father's new girlfriends. Not long after our divorce, he had a new wife and three children. They did not last long. And the hardest part was that this father abandoned our daughter, blaming this five-year-old girl for not maintaining their relationship.

I applied for and obtained my first job in years as a custom decorating consultant for a major national department store chain. I began the demanding new life of a single working parent. The paperwork connected with the drapery design work had to have been issued by the government. It was grueling in its specificity and complicated layout. I was terrified I would make an error.

I was exhausted and guilt-ridden about the adjustments my little girl had to make. The battle over visitation and child support was fierce. Everyday maintenance of life, trying to hold on to a normal home life for my child, took a toll on my body and mind. With all the pain and trial of my new life, it was not as terrifying for me as being married. I could not function in the same town with him. I took my car in for repair. When I returned for it, the garage refused to release it to me. My ex-husband had not paid his bill. They thought they could hold my car ransom for his bill. My attorney changed their position for them.

I prayed to God to remove me from my ex-husband's reach. Then I did not wait for his answer. My landlady, who was initially friendly toward me, out of the blue terminated my rental agreement. I discovered later she had a friend to whom she wanted to rent the house. I found an apartment near the college and again had to uproot my daughter. I was barely settled there when an opportunity to move to a major West-coast city presented itself. It was a way out.

I took it without really looking at the situation or my motives for jumping at the chance to "cut and run." I flew my daughter back to see her grandparents while I dismantled our life and packed up my car and a small U-Haul, intending to travel alone to our new life. My parents would then fly my daughter back to me.

My dear minister friend decided that he was going with me to help me drive. I told him I could do it myself. He insisted it was too dangerous for me to be out on the road with an older car and a loaded trailer. We arrived safely in the city, my friend's hometown. He went to his brother's. My trailer and I went to share the home of a friend from my past and her thirteen-year-old daughter. I knew the moment I arrived I had made the wrong choice again. I had removed myself from the reach of my ex-husband, but into what had I delivered us?

Now I was committed. Working for the same company again as an interior decorator put me out on the road in a strange town winding through unfamiliar streets with a map in one hand, steering wheel in the other. I made four to five in-home appointments a day. I was stressed at work and stressed at home. I had to leave my child in the hands of a thirteen-year-old.

It all proved too much. I wound up in the hospital with full-body inflammation. After packing me in ice to bring down my temperature, the doctor performed surgery. He removed my infected gall bladder and appendix and did an exploratory for cancer. All this happened just before Christmas. I had planned to fly to the Midwest to be with my family for the holidays. I had flown my child on ahead. Eleven days after surgery I was on the plane. I was miserable, weak, and in pain but headed home for Christmas.

The harder I struggled to control my life, the more of a shell I developed. By now I was going to psychic healers. I had pain everywhere, and the healers were giving me relief for my aching body. This fueled my desire to find the answers for some peace in my life. I read books on tarot, read my horoscope daily. I bought books on defining myself by "my sign." I investigated Eastern philosophies and other religions, searching for confirmation that self was right. Self was the way to peace and success.

I lived in a state of constant stress. Two years after the gall bladder surgery, I developed kidney stones. I had blood in my urine, was cold and tired, and had a chronic ache in my back for a year. I worked, pushed, and drove myself through the pain. The doctor finally found a kidney stone the size of a large cough drop filling the vestibule of the kidney. This condition led to another operation and six more weeks off work.

I had reconnected with my cowboy, who was still not free. I could see the futility of the situation and did not want to live life on the fringe.

He continued to pursue me but wanted to keep his life intact and still have a relationship with me. It put a huge strain on my body having to go back to work too soon. I again asked God constantly for an answer. I just never listened. I was physically at a low point and running out of energy for dealing with my life. Why God wanted such a stubborn spirit is a mystery to me to this day. I finally gathered enough strength to move out of my living situation into an apartment north of the city. A week after I moved in I was caught off guard by a call from my ex-husband. He was in the city and wanted to take us out to dinner. I wanted to decline, but my little daughter overheard me answer the phone. All during dinner he told me what a wonderful job I was doing raising our daughter. Stress level was through the roof. I could not figure out what he was up to.

When we got home, he asked if he could come in. My daughter was so excited that I said yes and made some coffee. He put her to bed and read her a story. I was furious with myself for automatically fixing his coffee the way he liked it. My head was pounding with a mega-migraine. We talked for an hour, he left, and I have not seen him since that time.

I had no inner strength to handle his intrusion into my life. I should have stopped him at the phone call. Instead I allowed his presence to feed my child's fantasy about Daddy coming back. The whole incident made me sick for a week. I dealt with him using chaotic emotions, instead of the unshakable principles a relationship with Christ offers.

I continued to go downhill, and it was not long before I was too ill to go on alone. I needed my family's help. Despite my weakened state, I still had to be literally wrestled to my knees before I accepted God's answer. I did not want to leave. I wanted to stay and have it all work out according to my dream. God clearly said, "You must leave." I stood in my living room, resisting the idea of leaving. I begin to feel pressure on my shoulders. My knees buckled. I was forced to my knees until I cried out, "Yes, I will go." I broke down and cried for a long time. When I finally picked myself up off the floor, I was peaceful. Even though I did not want to leave, it had to happen. I resigned my position and made plans to go.

The day I was to pick up the trailer and load up my belongings,

I went to the bank, withdrew funds, and closed the accounts. Then I drove to the rental place to hook up the trailer. I had my purse next to me in the seat. The men hooking up the trailer took an inordinate amount of time at the task. Then they asked me to step out and go to the back of the car so they could show me the how the lights were hooked up. One man got into my car as I got out, saying he had to check something under the dashboard. I had used my credit card to pay for the trailer. I did not discover until I got home that all my money was gone.

I once again called out to God. "If you want me to go home, why are you throwing me roadblocks? Please give me the wisdom to handle this problem." I called the manager of the shop and told her what happened. I told her the amount of money that was missing and that it was all I had to make this trip. I begged her to help me. I spent the next hour in gut-wrenching panic, tears, and anger at myself for my naïve behavior. As of the next day I would have no home and a trailer full of possessions with a deadline for return. I would have no money with which to travel.

Finally the phone rang. The manager had called every employee in to her office. She said, "Give me all the money you took from the last client's car. Don't bother denying it, and don't make me call the police." She retrieved every dollar. She apologized, and asked if I would mind coming back to get it. She could not leave the shop. Sometimes I wonder how my adrenal glands have survived my life.

The next day I was on the road, this time with a larger tandem-wheel U-Haul, having flown my daughter back ahead of me. My mother had flown out to ride with me. My spirit was so rebellious that all I could think about was how and when I could move back to the West.

All my life, I had claimed to love God and had turned to him for answers. At the same time, I resisted his plan for me. Saddest of all, I never thanked him for all he had given me. It was all about asking for his approval of my plans, moving on my own feelings, and then asking for miracles to rescue me from some mess I had created.

I woke up the day after the long, tense trip pulling my life in the box on wheels. We unloaded all my belongings into the basement of my parents' home. I got in the car to return the trailer, and the car would not start. The alternator had died. If I had stopped at one more place along the road, I would still have been there. I called a friend with a trailer hitch to return the trailer. With the last of my trip money I repaired my car. I had no time to rest. I called the same company I'd worked for out west. I interviewed and got the job as custom designer.

Within two months I had moved into a duplex with my older sister and enrolled my daughter in school. I was back to work, this time in snow and cold. Life was not any easier at forty below zero. I kept on trying to control circumstances. For every five fires I tried to extinguish, a sixth would flare up and burn me. One lesson I learned is that we cannot pull a geographic relocation and expect life to improve, because *we are the unchanged common denominator in every move we make*.

I had to change if I was going to move forward. *If I had been really in tune with God, I would have known he wanted to protect me from a harmful situation. In true relationship, I would have accepted the move as his plan. I would have peacefully obeyed his decision to send me home and then listened to his plan for my life.*

I am sure it is apparent to you by now that I made my life very difficult. I worked at living much harder than I had to. I would not take opportunities to even look at what a life in Christ had to offer. Why are we humans so fearful of choosing to return to our Creator? Is it because we are born into a world which feeds our natural human self-involvement in every aspect of our lives? Almost every waking moment from our birth, along with our natural bent, we are receiving messages that we are the center of the universe. We are born as self-centered and self-gratifying beings. We are temporarily separated from God, born into a physical body with a human nature, separated in spirit from the God who placed us here. Many of us gain approval and praise for accomplishments of self. We are taught to make plans for our lives. Many good and loving parents neglect to instill in their children the most vital information to insure their safe passage through this life and their ultimate return to God for eternity.

It is different if we are born to parents who have a personal relationship with Jesus Christ, parents who raise us to believe we must praise and thank God for the gift of life and ask him what he wants for our lives—who teach us that without God we can do nothing and will spend most if not all of our lives filled with self-importance and pride.

We may or may not become "successful" by this world's standards. But unless we return to God through Jesus Christ, we are never successful at anything that matters. We come into this world naked and crying, unless we find the safety and comfort of relationship with Christ, we will leave this world naked and screaming, headed for a painful eternity.

We are a little like a kangaroo who is expelled into the world from the womb. Blind and an inch or so in size, it must hang on for dear life to its mother's fur, the only security it knows, until it can climb inch by inch to the protection of the pouch. There it is nourished and protected until it grows and matures. When it emerges again it is ready to face life with strength.

Our lives are filled with all that the world calls pleasurable and satisfying. We are led down many dead end streets with empty promises. We believe the world's promises which fill our hearts and souls with food that can only temporarily feed our senses or emotions. We lead undisciplined and self-indulgent lives. The longer we live this way, the more determined we are to make it work, to do things "our way." We spiral along, making up our moral code through a fog of self-deception. We grow demanding, controlling, and angry with anyone who stands in the way of our "happiness," stubbornly determined to prove our way is best.

Eventually, we pitiful, rebellious creations are brought to our knees. We answer the call of God with the full weight of our self-importance pinning us to the ground before our Father. If we are fortunate, it happens while we are still alive, giving us the chance to turn our lives around. And if we humble ourselves before him and accept his gift of mercy, we can become new creatures. We can enter into the life God meant us to live.

We must choose spiritual life over spiritual death. We must choose to be reunited with our Creator. It means giving up all of self. It also means gaining all of what we were meant to be. A love beyond all that we can wrap our minds around will fill all the emptiness the world or other human beings can never fill. So what are we afraid of? Are we afraid of letting go of the only power we know, our perceived "self-made" image? If we are taught from birth that we are in Christ, who is really in charge of our lives, we can ask direction minute by minute. We can have love instead of lust, joy instead of anxiety, peace instead of fear, the constant knowledge that we have a glorious eternal future.

If we are not taught about Christ from birth, we must struggle to accept God through his son. He knows where we are and is always there if we ask him into our lives. Looking for the perfect love? We can only find it through Jesus Christ and a humble and disciplined life. Humble means constantly being aware of who created us, praising him for the blessings no matter what form they take in our lives, in total trust. If we never have a problem, we will never experience the greatness of God. We will never know God. We do not have the capacity to understand him, no matter what our IQ. We can only "make sense" of anything to a point. Then we must trust in God. Read his word for direction, and accept his final word on the subject. We must recognize the limits of our human strength and be grateful for a God who is always with us. Only he can lift us to life on a level of positive, peaceful, productive pursuits.

Without him, we are burning ourselves up, overwhelmed with busyness. Flailing motion is not progress. Are you reactive or proactive? Is your life ruled by what is coming at you, or by how you are coming at life? Who is in charge of your life? When God is in the lead, you are elected, directed, and protected. If you are swimming around in a fishbowl bumping into the glass trying to find a way out, look up; the only way out is up.

When we take our place in the order of the relationship God has designed, everything in our lives begins to come into alignment. Chaos may surround us, but we are in the eye of the storm where calm prevails. We have to choose to step back into the storm.

Two years was all I could stand of the winter weather. In addition, my hometown and I had not changed together. I longed for the West, for the mountains and the ocean. Again I rebelled, determined to make my dream work. We moved back to the Northwest. I found a wonderful house to rent and a job close by, and we began our second life in the West.

The company I went to work for appeared to offer a solid

opportunity. It turned out to be an empty promise. My parents and oldest sister had by this time moved to town. I decided to go out on my own and open a business. I was not the kind of "entrepreneur on a shoestring" who sold her Arabian horses and two of her luxury cars to scrape enough money together to start her business. I took a flying leap off a cliff with two months' savings. I placed ads and called a list of former clients. Like a fledgling, I plummeted downward, flapping my wings furiously until I cleared the rocks on my way up.

In an effort to give my daughter exposure to God, I joined a start-up church in our area. She joined the youth group and seemed to take to the world of "church life." She attended church camps and made mission trips to inner-city areas. She participated at the national level in our denomination. I became involved in the growth of our church. I was serving on the board when we began the building project for the physical facility. I threw myself into the effort with my usual commitment and controlling practicality. I did not have the right relationship with God through Jesus Christ. I was again attempting to bring human reason to what I perceived as a classic case of religious myopia. Contracts were signed which clearly benefited the contractor. They were seen by the rest of the board as "covenants," but they were custom-scale prices paid for simple stock plans for the building. It all proved too much for me to accept. I could not understand how intelligent people of the community could lose their acuity and business savvy when it came to the church. They were acting on a kind of faith that was not familiar to me.

After the church was built, the minister began to introduce butterflies, balloons, and games into the Sunday services. He was an artist. He led the congregation in a carnival atmosphere, placing emphasis on the celebration of food and fun. One Sunday we came to church to find kazoos under each seat. I had convinced my parents and sister to join. We were all founding members. I spent most of my time in that congregation frustrated and empty. Eventually I drifted away. During that time, a friend asked me to come to her church with her. I avoided the issue after I found out it was a Baptist church. I just did not want to go through another session of someone trying to wash me in the blood.

Disillusioned and tired of people in general, I decided not to be involved in anything for a while. I needed time to think and bring God some more plans for my next phase. I cannot believe, as I write this, what a slow learner I was. There I was, hanging out in limbo, exposed and unprotected, licking wounds and needing something to work out. If ever there was a mind absolutely ripe for the picking, it was mine.

I am not really clear on what brought the issue of child care to my mind. The safety, protection, and nurturing of children has always been a strong desire in my heart. The enemy filled the void. He had found someone to devour and had the perfect plan to fill my need to solve problems, a plan to cater to my need to protect, take charge, create, and shine. His triumph in my life was delivered as God's plan for me.

I became very quickly and powerfully impassioned about the need to give the world excellent child care. I began to design the kind of space children need to have. Soon the project took on a life of its own. It consumed my life. Ideas started coming so fast. People came into the project seeming to be heaven-sent. All the "coincidences" fueled my desire to take on an enormous project way beyond my human abilities.

People with strengths I did not have began to join the march. Soon the friend I had first stayed with brought her skills as a nurse to the project. I was led to investors, who began to fund the project. An architect/contractor was introduced. He worked for very little money because he saw the potential and grasped the concept.

During this huge project I needed to make some immediate money for living expenses. I designed a support business for real estate offices. The work required three or four hours of my time at night and then two hours of driving time five mornings a week. It ballooned into more routes than I could handle. I enlisted my parents, my daughter, a friend, and my nephew.

Every night I would fix dinner while they collated the work and set up the routes. The next morning we ran all over the city delivering flyers and picking up the next day's work. Four years of my life were spent on the child care project. It proceeded all the way to blueprints of the physical plant. We developed policies and procedures and designed forms and legal documents. We bought the property and finalized all plans from the building to the services.

Then, as suddenly as it formed, it all flew apart. The investors asked me to jettison my original partners. Because of my misguided loyalty, I could not do it. What had started out to be care and concern for children turned into a high-end care center for the privileged children of professional couples. The project was focused on profit and prestige.

What I thought was God's plan for my life I now know, was the work of the other side. All of the "falling into place" and "magical appearances," the "signs" of just what was needed, all of which I had attributed to God, was Satan at his finest. I might just as well have signed a contract in blood.

I believed in what I was doing. I pushed on, struggling through many personal and family issues during that time, even taking a close relative through treatment, all the way from intervention to clean and sober. I could no longer carry the load. All the plates were spinning on the poles. More poles and plates appeared, and plates began to fall. Finally it was all washed away in one giant wave of betrayal, trickery, and punitive disloyalty. I stood in the middle of the destruction and could not understand why it had gone so wrong. I believed completely I was following God's leading.

Today, more than twenty years later, standing on this side of the chasm, I know exactly what happened. Satan is more than able to draw us into his world. All he has to do is use our own pride-filled selves against us. When we do not have God's standards ingrained in us or Jesus Christ as Lord of our lives, we have only our pitiful ego as a weapon of defense. We are open to evil flattery and easy manipulation. I was devastated and brokenhearted over the disintegration of a dream into which I had poured my heart, mind, and money. Why, when the intentions were so good?

One of the personal problems that erupted at this time was the next reconnection with the man who swirled in and out of the background of my life. We had not even spoken for five years. I heard he was having a difficult time. I wrote him a letter offering to help if there was anything I could do. If not, he did not have to respond. He called. That began another phase of making choices that eventually ended painfully.

My attempt to accomplish something seeking God's approval had failed. I fell back on a familiar pattern of "helping" to solve someone else's problem, instead of looking at how I had participated in my own load of loss. I lost the property, the project, the partners, and everything I had invested. Most regrettably, I lost time with my daughter and family. I wanted so much to gain the approval of God and those who knew me. I sacrificed time and relationships to achieve temporal "success". I moved in temporarily with my parents. I began to focus on other people's needs, not from my heart, from my ego. This is not the way God tells us to give our lives in service to him.

Soon, by mutual agreement I was deeply involved in relationship with my cowboy and his life. I had skills and knowledge that were a help to him in dealing with a very ill wife. We worked together to do our best to make her as comfortable as we could. She entered a nursing home in a vegetative state. We moved on with our lives, together.

This is the "Cliff Notes" version of a long and complicated chapter in my life. Details would only cloud the issue. I want you to see how we humans twist, turn, and justify our decisions. We override even our most basic sense of right and wrong. We want to make our lives work out the way we envision them. In our minds we deserved some happiness, after everything we had each been through. Now, you understand that what we had both been through was a direct result of our own choices. With each choice, we constructed a set of justifications for our actions. That allowed us intellectual peace in the "after all's" of this kind of thinking.

Only because of repentance and forgiveness from God and my acceptance of salvation am I able today to honestly look at how separated from God I had become. Without Christ as my guide, I again believed what I was being told and what I was telling myself. Again the pattern of comfortable choices operated to engineer the outcome. I had just been through darkness on earth and had learned nothing. What was worse, we believed this was what God had ordained for us. Being together was our reward for enduring all the horrible problems life had dealt us. Are you beginning to wonder why God even bothered with me?

As you can see by now, you do not have be, as some people believe, a category-five sinner. We do not have to be elevated by Satan to all of the top ten sins to be a sinner. Separation from God at any level or to any degree is sin. And the "Amazing Grace" part of it is that, no matter where we are on the downward spiral, he is there to receive us, right up until that flash between life and death as we understand them.

We were convinced of our future and moved forward. We knew we had little family support for our decisions. We also believed that all those who opposed us viewed us through their own agendas. We knew we had to leave in order to find our own life together. We decided to take a vacation and talk about where we wanted to live.

CHAPTER FOUR

WILDERNESS: DISGUISED AS BLISS

W e were persecuted by family members for our relationship, labeled and criticized by friends because my cowboy was still married. Even my daughter said she shared information with me which should have halted my decision to be involved with this man.

I have no recollection of that warning, an issue which strained our relationship for years. I later had to seek professional help to try to face what I had blocked in my obsession. When we human beings are literally, "Hades bent" in our determination to do life our way, we are blind and deaf to anything that threatens to derail our plan. We are as blind we as we are to God's truth when it is presented to us. Despite all the opposition, we pressed on. We decided we were up against a wall of opinion with which we could not make peace. We removed ourselves from everyone's reach and anger.

We made a trip to another western state. My significant other's hometown was celebrating an all-school reunion and state centennial celebration and we wanted to see if we might want to live there. We planned, after a seven-week stay, to move there and start our new life together. We lived together, unmarried, for seven years. After his wife died, I still did not want to marry him. Marriage was still so frightening to me that I saw no sense in possibly destroying our relationship by legalizing it. I convinced myself that marriage was a legal-contract choke hold, almost impossible to break if one or the other wanted out. If love could not hold us together, then what good was a paper?

Eventually he convinced me. He wanted to make sure I was taken care of when he died, and marriage was the way to do that. I consented to a civil ceremony. We seemed to be very happy. I know I was and assumed he was since he told me daily in every way that he had never been happier. He said he "did not know people could live and love so peacefully together."

We had chiseled out a circle of friends, most of whom were summer people. We did not need too many people in our life. We were content with each other's company. We loved the slower pace of life and were very happy to be away from the large population of a city and family politics.

We saw tremendous potential in the town and began to purchase real estate. The town had offered me the job of planning director for the valley. For one year I poured effort and energy into trying to organize the community and move it forward. That was what I was hired to do. The problem was that only a handful of people were interested in their future. The rest wanted no change. A year later I was out of a job to which I had given my best. The town council decided new chairs for the 100 year old asbestos-riddled town hall were more important than the future of the town.

My daughter had by this time moved to town, obtained a job, and started a life. My husband and I opened a shop selling local artisans' work. It soon grew to 85 contributors from all over the country. We bought a couple of homes and turned them into vacation rentals. All of these moves brought enemies and hatred.

The next move was to become a real estate agent working for a broker friend. This brought more anger, lies, and rumors from the community. None of it really mattered to us. We attributed the negative feelings to the people's lack of education and motivation. My attitude was this: The properties we purchased were all here ready for purchase or promotion long before I came. If the natives did not pick up the options, they had no one to blame but themselves. I was privately sarcastic and arrogant about what we had gained. And right on schedule, it all began to unravel. The utilities took a 50 percent hike. The town's largest employer shut down, and the mines closed. All this took its toll on our rentals and the gift shop.

About that time my father had a brain stem stroke. After many trials with the medical community, we finally received a correct diagnosis and abilities assessment. We determined we would take him home to be with his family. This required 24/7 care and took my focus off business. We sold off properties as quickly as we could and tightened up our living. My husband and I were now sleeping in the building that had housed our gift shop. We turned our home over to my father and mother. Eventually we found them a house in which to live that did not require harvesting wood for heat.

His 24-hour care continued for a total of two and a half years. It was our privilege to care for him. My sisters supported our efforts as they were able from long distance and visited as often as they could. They were on call if they were needed. My father had devoted his life to his family and their happiness, always denying himself and sacrificing for us. Having him safely with us was a blessing.

During my father's illness, I began to have significant pain and hemorrhaging. I let it go too long, thinking it was just part of menopause. When the report came in, it was cancer. My daughter was about to deliver her first child. I was headed for a hysterectomy, six weeks of radiation treatment, and a radioactive implant. We commuted 130 miles to the hospital, one way. We were home on the weekends and back to the hospital every week for five more days of treatments. My first grandson was born during the treatments, and we made it to another hospital 30 miles away in time for the birth. There was no time to rest. Dad could not understand where I was, and I needed to keep going for him and my mother. I kept praying to God through all the trials to give me the strength to keep going.

The radiation made me very weak and tired. My father died in January of 1995, in his usual organized and gentle manner. We surrounded his bed, telling him we loved him and what a wonderful father, grandfather, and husband he had been. *The local pastor who performed the memorial service did not address the issue of salvation. He never asked if my father was a Christian. It was assumed that he was with God. If anyone could be there based solely on their own merits, my father was there. I did not know if my father was reborn. I remembered my dream at fifteen and comforted myself that he had made it into heaven.* My mother moved into one of our rental homes. Three years later we moved her to the northern part of the state to live with my oldest sister, in the same town with my younger sister and her husband.

My second grandson was born almost year to the day after my father died. The boys were a blessing and lifted our spirits in a time of difficulty.

My husband and I moved ahead with continuing health problems for both of us. Through all the stress, I had started selling things on the Internet to bring in some income. I also served on the county tourism board twelve years, a position that put me in touch with people statewide who were interested in bringing new people to Wyoming for recreation and or relocation.

The locals did not want people to discover their private playgrounds and towns. This brought more hateful remarks and actions to my doorstep. We were invited to visit a church, but we had no interest. I felt as though I had failed at everything I was sure God had directed me to do. It put me into the spiritual doldrums. How could I any longer go to God, when I had so badly carried out all my plans? I had wasted any talent or gift he had given me.

I was very involved with my grandsons and loved taking care of them. I considered myself a very fortunate grandma to have them in my life almost every day. Crises small and large continued to batter our lives, keeping the stress level high and corrosive. However, nothing appeared to damage our marriage. We worked through whatever happened and seemed to be solidly together.

Then without warning things changed between us, slowly at first and then accelerating rapidly. The details of my husband's betrayal are not necessary to reveal. I will tell you that world-wide participation in computer card games, such as cribbage and hearts, is a virtual portal to a very disturbing world of online experiences. On the surface he was as attentive and affectionate as always, but wives know. Even if some act as though they are dumbstruck and clueless, they know the minute it starts. Denial is just a safe place to hide from reality and appear a victim.

It took a few months to gather the evidence. Even with hard evidence in my hands I did not want to believe it. I was so wounded, I wanted to die. After giving him many opportunities to come clean and confess, the moment came when I could no longer listen to the lies. I confronted him. It was St. Patrick's Day at noon, 2003. His immediate reaction was to totally deny the accusations. He claimed innocence, attempting to convince me I was not in my right mind. Insults to my intelligence and accusations of lying were cuts I did not expect. I waited until he had firmly taken the stand of falsely accused, and then I presented the evidence.

At that moment, as I looked across the table at the rapidly draining face and shocked expression, I felt rage building in my recesses. I was primed to explode with words and threats that could never be retrieved. That was the defining moment that began my run to Christ. I looked down at the floor and saw nothing but blackness. I screamed inside, *No, I will not let this destroy me. God, help me handle this devastation. I am so scared. I have to forgive him in order to survive, and I can't forgive him without you.* My stomach was turning over and in on itself like boiling lava. The shock of losing the man I thought I knew and loved so much was tearing me to shreds. We were breaking into shards before my eyes, and we could never be put back together.

Betrayal from a person you trust and love is harder to live with than the physical death of that same person. There are identified steps in going through the grief process, and professionals can lead you through grief, if you are in Christ, he will take you through the pain.

Betrayal is an open wound with which you must live. Unless you forgive the betrayer, you will consume yourself with hate, anger, and thoughts of revenge. I now realize my husband succumbed to his human nature just as I had done many times. He could not overcome the temptation and moved into a dark world. He convinced himself that it was just a hobby and should not affect our relationship. His hobby showed so little respect for females of all ages that it was impossible for me to see myself continuing in a relationship with him. All the years of loving him were sucked out of me in an instant. In my internal vacuum, all I could hear were the echoes of screaming and crying I could not vocalize. I had been in love with someone who did not exist except in my mind. He like many of us is the human definition of good and loving, but his particular weakness is very difficult to reverse, especially when he had no desire to reverse it. Then there was the larger truth I had to face: "If they will do it with you, they will do it to you."

In that terrible moment I grabbed upward for God's hand. That kept me from falling into a pit of anger and hatred out of which I knew I would never be able to climb. As I watched him, he reminded me of an astronaut working outside the ship that is suddenly released from his tether and floats away. His partner watches helplessly as he melts into space.

I began by making decisions exactly opposite from what my human nature felt like making, reaching for God at every step. I kept repeating, "Save me, God, please do not let go of me." In a stunned and deliberately mechanical manner, I laid out the structure under which we would be living. Until I could get my bearings, there would be no divorce. I had not worked for a long time. At fifty-eight, with multiple medical problems, I was not a prime candidate for the work force. I resisted the urge to throw his possessions into the street and run over them with the car. I told him where he would be living and how. Throwing him out of the house at eighty-plus years of age, with nowhere to go, was not humane, and I could not do it. He also belonged to God. In order to hold this situation to God's standards, we both had to somehow come through this as whole as possible.

The next day, I was exhausted from crying and thinking about the disaster that was my life. I shuddered at the thought of all the work ahead of me. In my broken state, I asked God to put me where he wanted me by my sixtieth birthday in December of 2003. I was done planning my life on my own. I thanked him for rescuing me from the darkness that had almost overtaken me. This was my first on-my-knees prayer to God.

My husband and I lived for a year in the same house, with rules of engagement. He did all the cooking, shopping, cleaning, and laundry. I had massive amounts of work to do to divide personal property, handle the legalities of our lives, and maintain sanity. This time, with God's leading; I laid out a plan for the reconstruction of our lives. During this year I handled the practical side of tearing my heart and home apart. God continued drawing me closer to his Son.

I wanted to leave town and never look back. I made a trip to visit my sisters and mother. While I was there I turned down a street unfamiliar to me and saw a for-sale-by-owner sign on a wonderful old log home. I turned in the driveway, drawn by a feeling of extreme familiarity.

Walking through the hedge gate, I stepped into a world of magical gardens, including a playhouse from the 1930s. There was a small log guesthouse in the back of the yard and an English garden of flowers surrounding all the buildings. A lovely shaded area with a swinging hammock beckoned from between two trees.

The inside of the house completed the vision in my mind of the perfect refuge from the world. I could see myself drinking tea on a cold winter night, curled up on the sofa, gazing out at the mountains. Even though the house was in the middle of the town, it was perfectly positioned on the property so that every window framed only the mountains. The foliage outside obscured any sign of neighborhood structures. I was shaking when I left. This was my house. I desperately worked every angle I could to see if it was possible to buy it, but I could not make it work. I wanted to run away from everything. Picturing myself in that house helped me escape my reality. When issues in my falling-apart life became overwhelming, I would put myself in my refuge. I mentally moved all my furniture and personal possessions into the house. It never became mine. It served a purpose in my transition and was, in a way, a foreshadowing of my future. Here again, for a moment in time, I became obsessed with engineering my own solution to a problem based on emotions. I asked God to make a way for my plan. I had said I was through planning my life, but giving up control was very hard.

I had struggled with sleep for a number of years, due mostly to physical problems. I had difficulty getting to REM and only slept for two or three hours at a time, unless I took sleep aids. I have always dreamt in vivid color, and almost all the dreams have a strong story line. In the summer of 2003 I began to have dreams on occasion that were dreary, dark and lacking color.

One dream stands out during this next transition in my life. On June 13, 2003, I had a dream that involved what can only be described as the demonic and torturous. I was the only human in the dream in which I did unspeakable things. Twisted things were done to me. I could not wake up. There was no color in the dream. A door opened into the room with light behind the man who walked through the door. It was my father, who at the time had been dead for more than five years. He appeared in a powder blue windbreaker, a soft yellow knit polo shirt, and gray pants. I could smell his aftershave. He looked like he did when he was sixty. He gave me a long hug, and his arms felt familiar. He said, "I am at peace and very happy. Do not give up. It will be hard; do not let him win." He was whole and looked wondrously peaceful. "You stay on the path," he said. He kissed my forehead and then disappeared.

Only then was I able to wake up. I did not know who he was talking about at the time. I do not interpret dreams, but I can tell you that I was deeply encouraged by his visit. It was comforting to know he was peaceful. He completely negated all that had occurred before his entrance.

I want to pause here to say again, I do not consider myself superhuman. The problems in my life are common in all our lives. Some come to us just because we are fragile human beings in a somewhat hostile environment of natural events. However, I believe most of our problems are a direct result of our stubbornly self-involved decisions. What I am trying to convey is how most of us meet the challenge. Not with cheap, shallow TV and movie versions of hedonistic stress reducers. Most of us just keep putting one foot in front of the other, returning serves as they come across the net. Sometimes this requires several racquets. We try to draw strength from friends, relatives, books, talk shows, and our own version of an Emergency God. We see fit to tap him only when we have exhausted every other way. We snatch words of "wisdom" from self-styled idols and newsmakers. Some of us have a belief in God as a consultant in our lives, there to agree with our solutions. Consider how it would be to have a solid core of belief, a source of unfailing power into which you were plugged continually. Every event in your life could be referred immediately to a source of strength and answers. You would be able to find a clear head in every crisis, guided by a love that holds you dear and never lets you go.

The next blow to my solar plexus came in the summer of 2003. Four months after I had confronted my husband. I called the United

States federal government, from which he had retired, to ask a question about life insurance. I was asked in an "oh, by the way" manner if I knew I was not named as my husband's survivor.

This meant I would not receive any retirement or medical insurance from the moment of his death. In the young man's next breath he said, "And now it is too late to correct the mistake." That problem added to the pile of disintegration with which I had to deal. I tried to find help through many legal sources. There was none available. I had to become my own legal representative and try to fight for some justice. I filed my case. I made my way through the maze of obstacles intentionally set up to discourage anyone from scaling the walls of Washington DC with justice in mind. I had to learn to jump through legal hoops, while learning the language of the law, which is no easy task. I persevered all the way to the point where I would have had to file with the Court of Appeals in Washington DC, appearing before the court to defend myself. I was physically, emotionally, and financially unable to finish the task. I asked for help from elected government officials with no resolution. I have been seeking assistance since 2003. I am still, into 2009, unable to be reinstated. I cannot receive what my husband worked more than thirty years for, as a government employee. I attacked the life-changing issue without my right relationship with God. I compromised more of my health. I spent sleepless nights and wretched days in a futile effort to "make it all work." Again, I tried to reclaim control of my situation. I had been retired for several years due to health issues. I was facing abject future poverty, alone. I was frightened. I had come closer to God but still did not have the faith and trust I needed. I was not in right relationship with Him.

Today I watch a new administration scatter unfathomable amounts of money like rose petals. Those in power feed those who put them in power. They call it "saving the economy" as if they had nothing to do with the collapse. As the ship sinks, I slip back into my human condition. Why did my husband who actually worked and contributed all his life, have to lose what he earned? Because of a technicality and incompetence on the part of the former employer, we lost earned retirement. *Once again, even though I had begun a better relationship with God, I did not trust him to lead me through this trial.*

A friend—I had met her six years earlier when I sold her a house—called me in August of 2003. My husband and I were living together and very few people knew our situation. She asked if I would come to a Bible class she was going to teach in September.

I have written the following story of our meeting to show how God puts people into our lives for his purpose. In a later chapter, another story tells how quickly he will remove the same people from our lives, again for his purpose.

My friend and her husband had come to our town from another state in 1997 looking for a place to buy. Her husband had wanted to live in Wyoming since he was a young man. A few days before, they had come away from a horrendous real estate debacle in the northern part of the state. They were headed home and stopped in a town twenty miles away to talk with a Realtor. When they inquired about real estate in a certain price range, they were politely told they should probably look in the next town up the valley, where they were more likely to find something in their price range.

Considering the rude treatment they had received earlier, it was definitely part of God's plan that they even stopped at my real estate office. We instantly bonded when I heard her approaching my screen door saying, "I don't know, maybe someone in here will talk to us." I said, as she approached the door, "Come on in, I'll talk to you." They were like old friends dropping in. We all felt a connection, as if this meeting had significance. They told me what they were looking for. I took them on my famous thirty-minute tour of the town, mixing history with politics and property that was available for sale.

As we turned toward the office, I suddenly said, "There is one more that is not on the market yet, and I don't know if it will be. My husband and I own it, and we have not made a decision about selling it. But since you are here, I will show it to you, if we do decide to sell you will have at least seen it." As we drove up the street, I pointed ahead toward the house. She said "That's it." She went through the house like a remote control toy car, darting in and out, extolling its virtues and taking mental ownership. I told them every flaw, pointed out all its idiosyncrasies, and kept saying, "Don't get so excited, I don't know if we are going to sell." She said, "You have to sell me this house."

I said, "I have to talk to my husband. You come over to our house after dinner and have some ice cream, and we will have a decision by then." They bought the house, and I was so pleased because I thought we would become good friends. We did spend some time together, Thanksgiving the first year and some evenings and dinners out.

As they became more involved in the community, they joined the Baptist church. Oh no!—they were *born-again Christians*. Even though I thought the world of them, I kept my distance to hide and watch. My friend tried on several occasions to talk to me about salvation, and I would have no part of it. I told her that I had a very comfortable relationship with God and did not see the importance of Jesus in that relationship. She tried diligently, even told me that it made her sad to think of never seeing me in heaven with her. She was evangelizing with great sincerity, and I was very uncomfortable with her questions and conversation. I deflected every attempt she made and then slowly backed away from spending too much time with them.

We still saw them occasionally and looked at the photo albums of their trips which I thoroughly enjoyed. I used to tease them about all the money they saved me, because the presentations of their trips were so complete, I never had to travel myself. The mission field was not something I agreed with. They had begun their mission work in another country. I could never understand why people of the world could not be left alone to live out their culture and religion and be appreciated for it. Full-blown "fish people"; too bad, because I really liked them.

CHAPTER FIVE

OUT OF THE
WILDERNESS

═══════

O ur visits over the next few years dwindled. By this time they were gone a good share of the year on mission. They were not aware that my life was coming unglued. God was working diligently in my life to bring me to my knees. It was in the midst of my greatest pain that the call came from my friend. She asked me to join a Bible study. And as we talked about it in the aftermath, we both questioned the sanity of her call and my response. When she prayed about whom to ask to the Bible class, God told her to ask me. She said Are you sure?"

When I answered the phone and heard the question, I heard someone say, "Yes, I will come. If I become uncomfortable I will not keep going, and you will have to accept that." When I hung up, I sat there slightly stunned. I had just agreed to go to a Bible study taught by a "fish person." God was on the move, and apparently this time he was not accepting no for an answer.

We were joined in the Bible study by a mutual friend. Together they bravely began to introduce me to the Bible. The mutual friend had been in the background of my life, the kind of friend who was always there and supportive. Over the fifteen years I had known her, we had never had to be in each other's pocket every day. I had great admiration for her. This Bible study came just before she was to move out of state. She was literally packing boxes and working on my salvation in a dead heat.

I made a list of reasons why I could not accept their position on Christ's importance in our lives. I was armed with a number of arguments people use to resist Jesus Christ, justifications to solidify their "highly intellectual" position. Here they are:

1. I did not ask anyone to die for me. It was not my idea for him to suffer; that was his choice.
2. God would not be exclusive; he would include all his people.
3. Too many people have translated the Bible, and it has too many contradictions.
4. Condemning souls to hell ... what kind of love is that?
5. Following Jesus equals not taking responsibility for your life and actions.
6. How can the Bible be relevant today?
7. I cannot commit to something I do not understand.
8. Following Christ means you have to give up all the things you love to try to attain perfection which is impossible.
9. Maybe Jesus Christ was man's invention, to sell a pathway to God.
10. Why can't we just cut out the middleman and have a direct relationship with God?

During that first day of study, they gave me a paperback Bible. They patiently tried to answer my questions. I could not understand the truths with which they were countering my position.

I could not understand because I was trying to grasp God's freely given gift with my microscopic speck of intellect instead of my heart. I likened it to standing on the other side of the wall, bumping up against it trying to find the entrance. They were shouting from the other side, "Just walk through the wall" in total faith. I wanted to, but where was the logic? I wanted to first be able to understand everything required in the commitment. They said, "You cannot understand it. You must accept the gift of God's love, trusting him completely. When you are over here, you will understand. God opens your heart and your eyes."

I loved God. I believed I had a perfectly good relationship with him. I truly desired to be able to read and understand the Bible, but my every attempt to do so was like trying to listen to a radio program with mind-blowing static interference. I was trying to end-run this Jesus part. I just wanted to read God's word.

I know I frustrated my friends beyond measure. They kept on, but it was like trying to push concrete through a cake decorator. As they said afterward, "It was like being midwives at a breech birth." I seemed to know instinctively that, once I stepped off that cliff and committed to trust God through his son, I would never be able to go back to the me I had created.

My pride said, "What if they are wrong?" Then for the first time in my life another voice in my head said, "What if they are right?" Still there was this huge issue of Sin. Original sin, born in sin, so defeating a concept, so inescapable and condemning an idea, how could a loving God use such a heavy and unredemptive hand in dealing with his children? I had seen the damage that kind of treatment inflicted when used by human fathers on children entrusted to their care. My friends pressed on, trying different avenues of approach. Nothing they were saying made sense. I went home from the first class, wondering if I should just call and tell them I did not want to waste their time.

I decided to go one more time. I had written down a few more questions based on what they had tried to tell me. The questions did not come in attack mode. They were questions asking for clarification. I found myself listening to the answers. The first time I was more concerned with rebuttal. Now we were discussing the issue of being a sinner from birth, the hardest concept for me to accept. How could you be a sinner, when your life had just been ushered into the world?

Then in one explosion of clarity came the key—a clear definition of sin. God, through my friend who was moving away, said, "Replace the word *sin* with the words *human nature*." **In that instant, I got it.** Her definition of sin began the toppling of the carefully measured and placed dominos of my defense. They began to give way at light speed.

Sitting there in stunned silence, I suddenly knew. Sin is not a third reality; there are only two realities: God's way to eternal life with him in heaven—and the way of human nature which leads to spiritual death for eternity in. It is not human beings who sin against God by doing things. We sin by being "fully human." Our egocentric nature separates us from God.

People naturally make choices on fear-based human feelings and concerns. Renewed souls make choices based on the principles and promises of God. *We humans naturally separate ourselves from God.* We must constantly choose, minute by minute, to remain in the will of God rather than following our human emotions and desires. We do not give up our human emotions and desires; we learn to control and direct them, God's way.

My perception of Christianity did not matter, as I saw it manifested in others. What mattered was what God intended Christianity to be: our personal relationship with him through our commitment to follow Christ. I was so stunned with the aftershocks of that shift in my thinking that I could only sit there like a donkey who had been hit with a two-by-four. Atoms and cells were lining up, creating loud noises in my head. My friends looked at me and then at each other, saying, "She just got it".

I looked down at the Bible in front of me and began to read through the tears welling in my eyes. I saw the word of God and understood it. We humans cannot possibly read God's word with clarity until we read it with our heart and head in sync. That moment of climactic understanding was only the beginning. It took my breath away and exhausted me. Tears rolled down my face. I knew my life had turned a corner. From that moment on I could not get enough information. Once you catch the spark, you cannot wait to surrender your life to Christ. The desire to know more, to go deeper into this absolute trusting relationship, truly is a consuming fire.

All of that happened in the first two sessions. On the day of the third class, my friend gave me a hardbound NIV Life Application Bible. She also brought another book that opened a whole new world for me. That book explained the physical structure of the Bible, how to read it, and which books contained what information. I treasure that little book. It is so clear and made my journey to reading the Bible so easy. Between my revelation, that book, and the notes at the bottom of each page of the Bible, I began to read and understand what I was reading. No more confusion and frustration.

I am not saying my intellect dissected each word. The words *Biblical Scholar* did not appeared emblazoned on my forehead. My heart heard. I read and understood the conceptual message in each book. As I read Genesis, it explained creation in his word in a way I could grasp it. It was all I needed to know. We could not possibly cope with the infinite details of any of God's creation because our brains are not big enough to contain and process it all. The average length of a human life does not allow us time to understand it all. I am not sure we were ever meant to do so. God gave us his word. It contains enough information to establish the foundation of our existence. He gave us our survival instructions. We must take all he gives us on faith, and then get about the business of living life by his word.

One evening after Bible study, I had to take my "husband" over the mountains to the hospital. That night, as I drove back over the pass, I stopped at the top. I looked at the full moon and the magnificent scenery bathed in its light. I had been thinking about the phrase "turning your life over to Christ." To me it had always meant acting irresponsibly and then asking God to fix it. Suddenly more pieces fell into place. The phrase really means making a commitment to follow what we know God expects us to do in every decision of our lives—even when it is what we don't want to do or something we have no experience doing, and cannot envision ourselves able to do. It means believing the rock will come up to meet your foot every time without fail. I started down the pass, tears running down my face. I was very excited about changes in my thinking. I thanked God for loving me so much, for sending his son as a sacrifice, and for his suffering the punishment I deserved.

All of these changes were being made while I was making arrangements to send my husband to live with his daughter. I was in pain and sorrow over the loss of love, relationship and the life I thought I had shared with him. At the same time I was filled with such joy at the anticipation of my entry into a life in Christ. Even though I lived in the same house with my husband, I never said a word about what was happening to me. I later came to understand how wrong I was not to have tried to involve him in the experience. I will never forget the agonizing 60 mile trip to the bus stop, and watching him walk up the steps and disappear into bus. I did not know if I would ever see him again.

After four sessions of Bible study, I felt I was ready to make my commitment to Christ. My friends were astonished at how rapidly I was understanding and believing what they were helping me learn. I was astounded at the speed at which my heart and mind were making course corrections. I was changing rapidly and felt as if I had connected back to that teenaged me who had caught the fire of service one night in a youth group, back when I first wanted to answer the call.

On September 26, 2003, I made what I thought was a sincere attempt at repentance. I praised God and thanked him for never failing me. I thanked him for never giving up on me, hard case that I was. For all the difficult, painful, but loving lessons he had given me, for carrying me, attempting to lead me, patiently waiting for me to turn my life over to him. I thanked him for instructing my friend to take the chance of stirring my sarcastic wit by inviting me to a Bible study. For adding a second friend, whose influence had even greater credibility for the study, and not adding anyone else to the group. For knowing the final tumbler to fall, turning me to his son, could only work if the people who came alongside me were people I felt I could trust. This was no coincidence. This was God's plan to bring me on home to fulfill his purpose with my life.

That morning I surrendered my life to Jesus Christ with what I truly thought was total release. I was anxious and excited to be reborn into my new life. I chose early morning because it is my best time, and there are no interruptions. I bowed my head and prepared my mind by praying the Lord's Prayer. I then surrendered everything. There was silence in my head. Then I heard, "*You and I both know you did not surrender all. When you are ready, I will be here.*" I was embarrassed and prideful as I stood up and shouted, "I turned my life over to you, and you rejected me. I do not know what you want."

Then the wrestling match began between old me and almost-new me. My pride, arrogance, and "do it yourself or it won't get done" way of operating were well entrenched. "After all," I said, "God gave us a brain and intended us to use it. I need to understand what I am committing to before I can possibly call myself a Christian." I wrestled with all the phrases and words that stiffened the hair on my head when I heard or read them. The song "Amazing Grace" had always brought out anger in me. I could not understand how considering yourself a "wretch" could possibly be honoring to God.

I paced up and down and fought mentally to return to my old attitudes, saying, "They almost got me. I can't believe I fell for this. Was I so desperate to read and understand the Bible that I allowed myself to be tricked into faulty thinking?"

I prayed, "Jesus, if you are real, please help me understand. I do not want to be self-centered and self-important. I am so tired of carrying this self-imposed burden." There I hung, in midair—not completely who I had been, but not quite who I wanted to be, shedding tears of frustration and crying out to God that I wanted to be reborn.

I felt I was being ripped in half. At the last minute before entering the birth canal, I turned around. As I struggled for balance, everything turned over slowly in my head. All the fragmented phrases taken out of context from the Bible, plastered on road signs like the ranting of lunatics, suddenly made sense. The disjointed messages of repentance that I, in my arrogance and ignorance, had with such clever wit maligned ... those messages became simply the truth. I had attributed them to the "mindless fish people." How could I have missed all this powerful truth? More important, why did I not see all the times in my life when God was calling me? I could feel the part of me I had held back in my earlier attempt to commit, folding itself into the baggage I had willingly tried to turn over. I felt empty.

I had always believed that intelligent, sophisticated people had a more appropriate relationship with God. It was so much better than the "fish people" who sat back quoting scripture. "Go forth and multiply" and "the Lord will provide"—which appeared as license to take no responsibility, resulting many times in too many children and no money to care for them. "Do not store up treasures on earth"—which seemed to mean no goals, no skills, and no ambition.

The tug-of-war for my soul lasted all day and into the night. No one came to see me, and no one called. That alone was very unusual. Even though I had experienced such a profound epiphany in Bible study, I was having a difficult time holding my ground or gaining any. I could not talk to anyone. This was a deeply personal struggle, and I was not armed. The only thing I knew was that I had seen the prize in a flash of light, and I wanted it. I struggled on into the night, and finally, on September 27, 2003, at five in the morning, I made the connection.

In the darkest depths of the night, some hours earlier, exhausted, I made coffee and sat down at the table with the Bible in front of me. I felt moved to read and started with Psalms. After a few minutes, I raised my eyes from reading and thought about what I had sincerely attempted to do the night before. My last piece of fearful, willful intellect had tried to bargain with God. I had held back 5 percent of my human nature in case this was not the real deal. I could then grab hold of the 5-percent rope and haul myself back to the top of the cliff from where I'd made my leap of faith. I would then continue on my path, like a cat, having cleverly restored my pride after testing the theory.

I read Psalms for about twenty minutes. Then I folded my hands, bowed my head, and began to pray. "Dear heavenly Father, I have always viewed you as my creator, my friend, my consultant. The one I turned to for approval of all my plans and efforts. I was long on requests, and very short on praise and thanks. I viewed Jesus Christ as another child of yours—my brother, since we are all your children. I never understood Christ as Savior, the sacrifice for us all. I did not understand that he is fully human, fully divine. I thought that for me to be 'like Jesus,' you wanted me to be the caregiver, the problem solver, saving people from pain and suffering. I was making other people's paths easier, even if it cost me the gift of my own time here on earth. I had a major Jesus complex. Since he was clearly your favored child, I must have wanted to be like him. I was engaged in spiritual sibling rivalry for your attention.

"I want to take my place in your plan. I know now, I owe you all. If you can use me, I surrender all I am to you. Come into my heart and change me. I ask this in Jesus' name, amen." I got up from the table and settled into my living room chair, hands in my lap, and began to seek God with all my heart.

My God, My God, why have I forsaken you? was the question that hung in the air above me in the dark silence of my living room. I was sitting in the dark seeking my redemption. This was the most important decision of my life: the acceptance of Jesus Christ as my personal Savior and Lord of my life here on earth and my eternal life. I finally understood what it meant to come to the end of self.

For the next two and a half hours I was suspended in a void, unable to move. My eyes were closed, and my chin was on my chest. Not afraid, but immobile and painfully aware the personality created out of my human effort and experience was dying and sloughing away. I would never be the same. I was saying good-bye, a piece at a time, to the me who would no longer have control of my life; I was letting go of all the stored pain I had concealed in an emotional time capsule. I sobbed until my ribs felt as if they were ripping away from tissue. My lungs struggled to draw my next breath as I remembered the death of my son over thirty-five years before. I had placed his death in a box and neatly stored it on a shelf in my mind to be taken down at some future date when "things settled down." Then I would examine the crisis of that horribly frightening night of blood on the white tiles of my bathroom. I knew the time had come to take down the box and relive the experience and give it to Jesus Christ.

In my immobility and exhaustion, I began to trust and turn over years of suffering of all kinds. I asked for forgiveness for all the sins I had committed against others, for the anger, impatience, sarcasm, and pride with which I dealt with people and events. I thanked God for all he had given me and for his unfailing love.

At times I heard my voice sounding like a little child. I turned over all the perceived personal power, all the guilt, frustration, and anger in which I sheltered and justified myself. Everything was laid down. Between the tears and exhaustion I was aware of being in-filled with a warm newness in every empty space. The process seemed to advance in slow motion. It allowed me to adjust to and feel every part of the experience. Each newly filled space was sealed in absolute trust.

I could never go back to what I had been. My rebirth was not a time of learning to love God, but of coming into right relationship with him through his son, Jesus Christ. I was beginning to understand who God really is and how highly he values us. The core of me belonged to God. We reviewed my life from birth to my then fifty-nine years of age in order to answer my question of why I had forsaken the one true God in favor of my creation of God.

I turned many more things over to God in that two and a half hour process of total surrender. Asking forgiveness from specific people I had hurt intentionally, giving all my guilt, pain and fear over to God, asking him to forgive me for not coming to right relationship sooner. Each issue of my self-directed life was displayed in my mind as an object in the small hand of a child. Her hand unfolded to reveal its contents which then floated out of her hand, and burst like a bubble. I was experiencing different intensities of tears during this surrender, which was so cleansing. When I finally stopped, my eyes still closed, I sat in silence and thanked God for his gift of salvation.

I could not move for some time, I don't know how long. I finally got out of the chair and slowly moved through my house looking at and touching familiar things. I was trying to anchor myself. Joy, peace, and relief filled me as I opened the front door to breathe in new air and greet the morning.

Dying to self has to be more frightening than physical death, because we are alive while we go through it. When we come out on the other side, we are still alive, only new. Still in a familiar world where we must live the same life as before, only now as utterly transformed people. It is an amazing experience to look in a mirror, see the same person on the outside, and know we are so different on the inside. We can no longer respond to or from old values and actions. We are new, and we have one person to rely on to rebuild our lives.

From that day forward, every decision in my day was challenged to meet a new standard, from the smallest to the largest issues of life. Television shows I enjoyed the week before, I now saw in a new way. They no longer held my interest. Comedians who were hilarious to me the week before, to my surprise, just made me feel sad when I tried to watch them. In my former life swearing was sprinkled colorfully through my conversations, especially in a humorous way. Now I could not swear without feeling a thump upside my head. And when I thought about all the times those words had come out of my mouth, tears would well up. My grandchildren, a few days later, observed that I was "calmer" and "not so nervous and tense." I slept better and woke up each morning smiling and excited about what the day would bring.

Every single aspect of my life became a relearning process. I had to put everyday maintenance of life into a routine, with regular hours for sleeping. It was a way to stabilize myself. I was a fractured person for many months. I continued to experience moments of "old creature," but "new creature" was gaining ground. I was shaking on the inside and fragile as I learned to walk the new path. I was taking in new information and revelations minute by minute, wanting to know more, and having to take naps during the day just to rest up for the next wave of information and change.

Since I was such a latecomer to the body of Christ, there was urgency. The process was in high acceleration. That was confirmed by Christian friends who said they had never witnessed such a powerful and speedy conversion. Everything seemed to come at me like I was standing on the finish line of the Indy 500.

God had answered my first honest prayer request in a swift and powerful way. I had surrendered my life to him in complete trust, and the joy was overwhelming. On my sixtieth birthday, in December 2003, God answered my March 2003 prayer. I was growing in my relationship with Jesus Christ, I was attending two Bible studies and tithing time and money.

My daughter thought I had lost my soul to a cult. I tried to talk to her, but she wanted no part of it. I had to keep moving on. I could only pray she would hide, watch, and eventually come to her own understanding.

God did not allow me much time before he took me up on my promise of surrender. He gave me an assignment of huge proportion. It seemed too large for me when I measured it against my self-perceived abilities. Then I remembered to trust. He was about to show me what is meant by knowing what it takes to follow Christ.

CHAPTER SIX

MILK AND FALTERING STEPS, A TIME OF TESTING

O ver the next few months I tried, haltingly, to gain strength. I reminded myself of a newborn colt struggling to get my legs, brain, and body all going in one purposeful direction. My missionary friend had started another Bible study. I eagerly joined five other women who met on Tuesdays. I was morphing in so many ways, still new to this business of openly studying and discussing the word of God. I was very quiet for the first few sessions. After all, it had only been a short time ago that this Book of Life was a complete mystery to me. I could not get my hands on enough information. I was meeting for the first time, in print and on television, powerful preachers who were teaching from the word. A television series presenting pure biblical teachings from a variety of excellent men of God became a favorite of mine—television evangelists who taught truth, not the "feel good about yourself, and have a positive attitude" preachers. I watched many others, some for a minute, and some for one show. I quickly weeded out what was not true to God's word. If a preacher only served up Bible light, I returned to the ones who also included God's perfect judgment. I felt like a wood chipper with branches coming in so fast I was exhausted trying to digest all the information. I was a baby Christian on milk and could not be filled. I wanted meat.

I went through my house searching out all the false information I had in the form of self-help books and tapes and all the false or distorted writings on Christ's teachings. All of it went to the dump. I could not give it to the library book sale or the thrift shops because I could not pass on information that would lead anyone else astray. I wanted to share all that I was learning with my family. I quickly learned what it meant to share my new life in Christ and have eyes glaze over and walls go up. I did get a positive response from my young grandsons and asked my daughter if I could expose them to what I was learning.

My missionary friend started a Bible study for my two grandsons. She was an excellent teacher. She put forth a great effort to have a lesson prepared for them each Wednesday and for our adult group every Tuesday. The boys were like sponges. It was a blessing for me to watch them not only understand but spontaneously create and perform skits based on the day's lesson. Those are memories I treasure more than anything the world could provide in the way of entertainment.

Everything was going along smoothly, and everyday living had a peaceful organization about it. It helped me gain strength and made me steadier in my walk. I began to contribute to the Bible study and felt more comfortable speaking and asking questions. I had a very strong need to have routine in my life through this period. I could not handle chaos; it took too much energy and changed my focus. I had not yet learned how to integrate a peaceful me into the fray.

My friend began asking me to go to church with her and her husband. She could not say enough wonderful things about the church she attended and the lack of strife in the congregation. I told her I was not ready for church, but maybe later. I had not been in a church for ten years or more. I was just becoming comfortable with what I was doing. Taking on a commitment such as church attendance was more than I wanted to do. God had another plan.

My friend finally set me up. She asked my grandsons if they would like to come to church the next Sunday to listen to her give a talk and show slides of one of their mission trips. The boys wanted to go. I was not going to stand in the way of them seeing the program. In retrospect,

I think it interesting she used the slide of a highly poisonous snake as the hook to entice them to come to church. I was uneasy at first, but the congregation was indeed very kind and welcoming. I began to attend with my grandsons on a regular basis, and I began to love Sunday mornings.

We were studying Job in Bible study. Between church attendance, visits with the pastor, and my new circle of friends, I was a busy spirit. I even attended adult Sunday school. I stood at the mirror on Sunday mornings at home and looked at myself. There I was, dressed for church and carrying a Bible, knowing this was who I really was. At the same time I wondered where the person had gone who laughed at people who carried Bibles. The boys would stay with me on Saturday nights for a movie and some ice cream. They kept their Sunday clothes at my house. Then we went to church and sometimes out for lunch or ice cream. I will forever cherish those Sundays with my grandsons.

I eagerly looked forward to the next Bible study, which would be the study of James. It was not long before God intervened in my life in a way I had not foreseen. Somewhere between Job and James my new life exploded. Through all the wonderful experiences with my friend the teacher, I had a feeling of hesitancy when it came to certain issues. I had told her I was gathering material to write a book. She had asked me to read a book she was writing. Then she asked if I was going to let her read mine. I said yes, but I kept avoiding actually giving it to her. Something told me not to let her to read it.

She asked me if I would do a sort of mini-ministry with her through the church. She had already structured it in her head and wanted to operate out of the church. She just knew we would be the perfect team. She told me she had never watched anyone move so rapidly into the application of God's word in their life. I told her I did not feel I was ready for anything like that. God's message of hesitancy, I thought, was not to be involved with her on any level other than where we were. I was definitely listening to Holy Spirit when I held back certain things about my life and myself. It would have been very like old me to share it all with someone to whom I felt so close.

That was not God's message. It was the message I had decided to hear. I did not want to totally disconnect with her because I was enjoying the learning. I had respect for her knowledge and ability to convey knowledge. I felt we were friends. We had the same sense of humor. We could finish each other's sentences and could talk for hours about many subjects. We joked about sharing a brain, but there was an inner tugging that nagged at me. Something was not right. Her attitude and actions did not always match her teachings. The idea that we must tolerate others' imperfections, combined with a works-in-progress mentality, served as excuses for not evaluating my relationship with her in truth.

God was telling me to end the relationship completely. What I did not want to give up, he dispensed with in short order. God was not teaching me about choosing parts of the relationship with my friend that I liked. He was telling me about my worship of her instead of his Son. That was what I was doing. I was regarding her as my conduit to God because she had been so instrumental in my salvation experience. I felt disloyal having uncomfortable thoughts about her. Even though other friends warned me about her, I defended her. I never considered ending the relationship.

The day came when she made uncalled- for personal comments about the pastor and his family to one of his close friends in the congregation. That person felt the comments were divisive enough to warrant telling the pastor. The exchanges between my friend and members of the congregation heated up, and within a forty-eight-hour period the battle was on. This peaceful and loving church family had a grenade lobbed into their midst. They had no time to decide how to defuse it. It became an irrational barrage of verbal gunfire in almost no time.

I had not attended church for a few weeks due to a family emergency. I was not involved until my friend involved me by telling me her side of the story. I was still on the outer edge of it, encouraging her to go before the board and explain her position. She refused to go and talk with the board or the body, even though she was invited to do so. The board finally decided to follow Matthew 18 in dealing with the situation. By this time the incident had taken on a life of its own. I was concerned about how this was playing out. I never intended to come out of my "comfortable Christian" position and get into the fray. I knew in my heart what she had done. I just kept praying for her to admit, repent, and seek restoration. God did not let me stay in my soft spot.

On the following Saturday I had an hour-long phone conversation with my friend. After the call, I was working at my computer. God started pushing me. The Holy Spirit clearly told me to call the pastor. I resisted for over an hour. I thought, *I can't—it's his day off.—Not me, I am not getting into this mess.* In between restating several times what he expected me to do, God began messing with my head. It was impossible to continue the flow of my work. I went to the phone that minute and made the call. I had not wanted to call and I did not want to be considered a gossip or critic. God assured me that he would be with me. He insisted I call.

I apologized to the pastor for disturbing him on his day off. I told him God had clearly pushed me to the phone that minute to call. I did not want to get involved, and I needed to hear both sides. I had not been to church for a few Sundays, and I was accepting influence from other people about what was going on in and out of the church. Maybe I could help bring some clarity to the problem. He said he was glad I had called. He and his wife had been in prayer all morning over this situation and praying for answers.

I made an appointment to talk to him. I brought my concerns to him, which substantiated information he had from other sources. I wanted everyone to see the friend I thought I knew. I was also sure my friend owed some apologies. The day of our meeting the pastor did not grill me. He let me talk. He answered all my questions and explained church discipline (Matthew 18). I understood why it is necessary, for individual health and the health and strength of the body of Christ, to take someone through the discipline of Matthew 18.

The next day my friend called and said there was now a third person accusing her. She was maniacal in her pursuit to uncover this third person. I was so shocked at how my friend, who was leading and teaching God's word to so many people, could be so deep in denial and self-centeredness. My friend was scaring me. I was afraid for her on many levels.

Before my eyes, her character changed along with her presence. She wore me out with her diatribes, which lasted for hours. She made volatile statements about the church, the congregation, and individuals. Nothing I could say calmed her down or made her look at her part in the experience. Her position was that she had done absolutely nothing wrong. I pushed hard for her to vindicate herself by going to the board and clearing her name if she in fact had done nothing wrong. God was opening my eyes and the eyes of the congregation as to what he meant by false teachers.

The very next day she appeared at my door without even calling to see if I was busy or if I had time or desire to talk. My daughter was picking me up soon, but that made no difference to her. She sat down and began to grill me like a prosecuting attorney about what exactly I had said to the pastor during a previous conversation. She wanted to again go over the details of how she had been wronged.

My daughter arrived. Just as I was leaving my friend asked me point blank if I was the third person. Because I could not spend any more time with her, and I had no witnesses or help, I lied to her. I said, "No, but I will call you tomorrow." I told her I would come up to her house and talk to her. It was my intention to tell her about my part in the situation. The guilt of lying to her was becoming too weighty.

The next morning she called before I could leave to go to her house. She said, "I know you are busy, and I have things to do. Maybe this is not the best time." Then she continued to talk for two and a half hours. I was not willing to tell her, over the phone, that I had lied. I told that I would go through the process with her. I would stand by her and wait through the parts she must do alone with God. At her request, I described a little of what of I had experienced in the cleaning-out of yuck in my life, the very scary process of asking God to free me of all the parts of me he could not use. The true humbling of oneself to God is not clean, neat, or organized. It is hard and messy and takes your faith to depths and heights no one can imagine. When you come through it, you are secure in relationship with God and his son.

The whole painful skirmish culminated in a meeting at the church of about thirty people. With God's leading, I had asked the pastor to convene a meeting so we could put an end to this misery. I then called my friend and asked her to attend the meeting. I told her the infamous third person would be at the meeting. I asked God to help me convey his message to my friend and the other people who would be there. I prayed for his will to be expressed in all of us. Understand that I had not even attended church for over twenty years. Now here I was in the middle of a major crisis in the body of Christ. This was a huge assignment for a new Christian. I was very nervous. God promised. I was standing on that promise and asking for his leading every step of the way.

The congregation, the pastor, and his wife had all tried to resolve this by asking to meet with my friend. She refused. At 2 a.m. the night before the meeting, my eyes flew open and my head was filled with words. I stumbled to the computer and typed for two hours. Then in the morning I rearranged some paragraphs and asked God if this message was the right one. I felt peaceful with the final draft. I e-mailed it to the pastor. In the message I apologized to my friend for lying to her. I asked her forgiveness. I explained how her behavior was being viewed by the congregation and asked her again to humble herself and admit to her part in the situation. I was sure she would be willing to participate in the act of mutual forgiveness with her friends in Christ.

When the meeting was called to order, there were thirty people in attendance. My friend was not accompanied by her husband, who was the head of their household. She was accompanied by a close friend, who she knew would not question her position. The pastor began by telling everyone the meeting would be recorded and asked if anyone objected. He specifically asked my friend if she objected. She said she did not mind. The pastor stated the purpose of the meeting and asked me to read what I believed was the message God was delivering through me.

My friend met it with coldhearted stubbornness. She rejected all the others who tried to speak to her. The bottom fell out of my heart. It was very hard to watch this person sever all ties with the congregation she had so embraced. And it was very difficult to accept the clear message that this person—who had helped lead me to Christ, taught me so much about God's word, and been my friend—would no longer be in my life. She was so fully steeped in willful pride that she was willing to lose dozens of friends rather than humble herself, admit her part in this hurtful experience, and exchange forgiveness.

The following is an excerpt from the letter I read to her in the meeting:

> I am asking you to forgive me for lying in answer to your direct question of me on the day you came to my house unannounced. You did not call to see if I was busy or if I had time or desire to talk. You grilled me like a heartless attorney about what exactly I had said to Pastor during our meeting. You continued to obsess about the "third person," this powerful "accuser" that you had decided was the cause of all your problems. I was on my way out the door and did not have time or skill to deal with the emotional tirade that would have ensued had I told you the truth at that moment.
>
> I had other choices; I did not have to lie. I could have told you to leave, that I did not want to discuss this matter with you. I could have said, "Until you resolve this by dealing directly with the congregation in accordance with scripture and the word, I cannot discuss this further. But in a weak moment I resorted to a flesh driven response.
>
> I would grieve if we lose our relationship over your stubborn will. Your spirit must meet your highly developed intellect before your desire to minister to people will explode into useful service to God. You told me you have been praying over and over Psalm 139. He is answering your prayer. Please see that. You could not ask for a more loving body of Christ to help you than are in your life right now. We all love you in Christ. You are not going to be allowed to be one of God's disruptive children in his family. Your choice right now is to reach out to everyone here and accept the love that is clearly demonstrated—or cut yourself off from that love and run to a new church. Then go around that same mountain again.

God has promised to be with you and all of us as we go through this. Do not allow past hurts and failures to take this opportunity away from you. More will go with it than I know in my heart you want to lose. Choose to be loved and to love. If you do not reach for forgiveness, because of what God tells us in the Bible, everything will crumble from under you. You know that as surely as I know it. God said so in his word, and he never lies.

I am asking you to forgive me for lying to you by commission and omission. It does not matter why I did it, but it matters greatly that I did it. Humble yourself, be willing to be broken with joy because you are being called to do so by God. Know that God will be with you and with all the rest of your broken, cracked, and mending family standing with you, trying to help each other stay on the way. You played a part in bringing me to salvation, and I would never question your salvation, but I will step out and question your growth in relationship with Christ. Let God help us all through the process of growing in relationship.

My friend chose to continue the fight with members of the congregation and finished by standing up and dismissing the group saying, "It's almost seven o'clock, and I have to get to the grocery store before it closes." With that she turned and left the church.

One of the members of our Bible study and her husband had come to the meeting. She came over to me to offer comfort, even though I did not know her well. Through my tears I said, "I do not want to lose you too." She said, "You are not going to, so don't worry about it." That began a friendship that took us rapidly into a God lesson neither of us will forget, to be clarified in a later chapter.

I never saw my teacher friend again. Her Bible study disbanded because she would not let go of the issues and drove people away by constantly discussing the problem, trying to justify her actions. She made several attempts through another friend to contact me. I knew it was not what God wanted me to do. I had only peace when I listened to Holy Spirit and refused to take the bait. She lost church fellowship by withdrawing her membership. She lost friends and her other Bible study group. God took her out of my life as quickly as he had put her in. I felt very bad about my grandsons not having a Bible study. It could not continue under the circumstances. More than that, they had seen a side of Christianity that gave them the wrong impression of the life of a Christian.

Over the next few months I had a variety of physical problems directly connected to the accelerated learning process I was going through. I was being taught how to discern the parts of life in my jurisdiction and the parts that belonged to God. It was not easy to rid myself of the long-established habit of trying to save everyone from everything. God was working in other lives too, and he would lead me to those with whom he wanted me involved.

The next three situations are examples that tested my ability to discern in accordance with my new commitment to serve God and not my ego. In rapid succession, people were brought into my life to present me with situations in which I would normally have taken charge or offered to "help." The Holy Spirit moved me to respond from a position of strength instead of ego, and I listened. In all three of the following incidents I began to learn who I had been and who I was becoming. In each case I was not unfeeling but very clear on what I could and could not handle. This was very much like homework.

The first note was addressed to a member of the congregation I had met briefly on a Sunday morning. I sat next to her a couple of times at a Bible study at the church. I had been cautioned by others to avoid getting pulled into her self-pity. I could feel her moving in on me. When she asked me to come to her house and visit her because she had no one with whom to talk, I declined her invitation to involve myself in her life. The old me would have succumbed to her neediness. She was revealed to me as an empty vessel only God could fill. I wrote the following with the intent of giving it to her. Holy Spirit said, "No, it is for you to read and understand. She would not understand it."

Note #1

I appreciate your invitation to spend time with you, but I am unable to do that at this time. I have prayed for direction in establishing new relationships, because I have in the past fallen prey to unhealthy ones. God has given me a clear message concerning you. It is a difficult one for me to relay. I have considered not relaying it and just distancing myself from you. God wants you to spend time with him in starting over on your walk. You know what God wants you to confess and correct. You cannot go on attempting to assimilate the relational experiences of others with Christ, as your own. God wants you to turn over your old habits and patterns of neediness and self-centeredness to him. You are sucking the life out of those who are trying to walk in love with you. You have mighty challenges to face in your life, as we all have. As Christians we are called to support each other. We are clearly instructed not to cause someone to stumble or to block the growth of another Christian's relationship with Christ. Enabling you to continue to operate in self, works against God's desire for you and would only keep you from going to God. We are called to speak the truth in love. The truth is you are exhausting an important source of potential love in your life. You are abusing the kindness and friendship available to you. We cannot choose our root families or the things of this world that come against us. We can make choices to seek to improve our attitude toward circumstances by choosing to draw closer God to truly listen and obey. I will continue to pray for you and your deliverance from the life of thinking you are a victim. A relationship with you now is not possible, but when you are ready to do the hard work of being honest with yourself and God, there will be many people ready and willing to come along side.

The next test came from someone I had known only as a nodding acquaintance at the post office or on the street. So it was a surprise when she called and asked me to pick her up at the garage where her car was being serviced. She was leaving town the next day, and she had no one to help her retrieve the car. This was another temptation for my ego to take charge and help.

Note #2

I picked you up at the garage as you asked me to, and we stopped at the store. We had a pleasant ride home. You are on your way out of town tomorrow to scout out a new life in another state. You mentioned you needed to have a huge garage sale. You said you wished it was in a better spot (red flag, my house is on the highway). I suggested you just go through everything and pull out what you wanted and put it in one bedroom. Mark everything else and leave it where it stands. Open the house, and have a sale. You then said what you needed was help (red flag); I did not respond. You mentioned that you had a lot of your mother's and grandmother's stuff and lots of tools. You did not know what those items were worth. That was a temptation of hidden treasure that "old me" would have had a difficult time setting aside. I did not volunteer to help, because I cannot allow unhealthy situations in my life. I need to learn when to help and when to stay out of things.

Users always state their case in a way that baits the codependent, controlling person into volunteering. I have to learn that it is my ego that takes the bait. Yes, I am blessed by God with multiple skills and talents. They all belong to him. God has me headed for a large project, and he bought and paid for all my energy and time.

Again, it was clear the message was for me, and she would not have received it. I never saw her again after I dropped her off at her house.

This last note was for a dear friend who attended Bible study with me. Her son had fathered a child with a woman who did not want the baby. She abused and neglected her. My friend was trying to care for the baby and eventually received guardianship of her. I did deliver this note to my friend.

Note #3

When you brought that beautiful little baby over to my house last weekend, I instantly fell in love. Holding her was a wonderful experience. I had not held a baby for a very long time. While I was holding her, I prayed for her and then was overcome with emotion. I cannot come even close to understanding the painful upbringing that can produce a mother who does not want her baby. She is hanging by such a thin strand in this world, but fully in God's hands.

You made the comment that it looked like you had "found another babysitter," and I did not respond to you. I couldn't. I thought if I were to take care of her for even one hour, I would become her rampaging advocate. I would do everything I could to get her out of her "mother's" hands. That was more of the "old self" than I could contain on my own. I have to learn what temptations will lead me back into the world of Super Women control. God wants me to completely let go of those old methods of dealing with people. Children at risk are my Achilles' heel.

I could not ask you to stay that day because I was on the verge of tears. They erupted like a bursting dam before you left the driveway. After many prayerful sessions with God, I believe I now have successfully turned the baby over to him. I can give her lots of love and attention when she is with me and put her back into God's hands. Now if you need me to sit for you, I can do it without running amuck, out of bounds, on a crusade.

I am absolutely sure of my salvation. I am also absolutely sure that it is not static. It will be tested and tried as it was being tested in these experiences. My relationship with God and Jesus Christ is more important to me than my relationship with my family. Asking Christ into our lives is a conscious choice. Studying the word is an organized, deliberate choice and can be done on our schedules. The growing in Christ is not organized.

Submitting to God's will is where we learn to let go and let God. We will find ourselves initially responding with phrases like "Not ready for this"; "Do not want to do this now, there's too much on my plate"; "Do I have to—?" As you grow, seek, and trust, it will not be long before you respond with praise and thanks to God for whatever he asks of you. This is how we find out who is really in control of our days and nights. It is how we learn to lay down a plan for the day and then learn to lay it aside when God calls. Then we pick it up again when we have done what he asked us to do. God does not ask more of us than he knows we can do with his help. We learn that we need Him to do anything well. He equips us and readies us for what He wants accomplished.

I enjoy public speaking. I can chair and conduct meetings and express myself on a range of subjects. I express love for family and friends openly with ease. Yet when I even think about trying to share the most important part of my life verbally, I become a deer caught in the headlights. I draw a complete blank. I am not able to quote scripture. I cannot debate or try to convince anyone with scholarly acuity that all the answers they seek are in a personal relationship with Jesus Christ. I do not seem to have verbal "Go ye" ability.

This may be because the subject is so intensely personal and important to me. I do not feel my voice can begin to impress the importance of salvation on anyone. In trying, I may do more damage than good. I can only try to describe in writing the exquisite joy and peace of totally surrendering our life to Jesus—the wonder of experiencing the transformation that takes place when we meet the real people we are in Christ. We come home to everything we have been searching for. Some of this we can define, an amazing amount of insight is suddenly new to us.

One of the great perks about doing exactly what God wants us to do is that we cannot fail. Imagine that for a moment … never having to worry about failing. That means we never fail as a human being unless we choose to do so. When we truly trust God the question is not "Why, God?" but "Where and when, God?" All-day communication with God is the power in our lives if we thank God, praise him, submit our petitions and end each prayer with "God, give me the strength to fulfill my part in your plan for this situation. In your beloved Son and our savior Jesus' name, your will be done. Thank you God, you hear and answer our earnest prayers. Amen."

It was not long before I was presented with another opportunity to witness for Christ. I had listed some property with a real estate company. It sold at a point in my life when I critically needed the money. I arrived at the title company a few minutes before the agent. We were joined by the closing agent. We chatted politely for a moment, and I said, "Okay, are we ready?" The agent said, "Yes, just waiting for your husband." I said, "He is not coming, he was not needed." "Well then, we can't close," she said. I told her I had a durable power of attorney and would be signing for him. She said she had no record of a DPA. All the paperwork was made out for both signatures. This was clearly the fault of the real estate agent. She knew she was responsible.

I had two choices at this juncture. I could follow my human nature and blow my lid, making the agent feel worse than she did for not seeing the way the contract was signed. She had also forgotten to attach the DPA to the paperwork. I could include the agent for not catching the signature on the contract. Or I could handle the situation in a Christ like manner, keeping everyone whole. A moment of difficulty, yes, as I turned my head toward the window, leaving two very uncomfortable people in silence, I asked God to help me do the right thing. I turned back and said, "Well now, there is always a solution. We are three intelligent women with a problem that must be solved. Too much is riding on this closing for me to leave here without my money. What exactly do you need to complete this deal today?" She said she needed an original DPA with original signature. She would have to redo the paperwork to reflect corrected signatures. "The original document is at home in my safe, and if I have to drive the 120-mile round trip to get it, I will. I believe my attorney, who is three blocks from here, has an original signature document. You call him, and I will call my daughter." My daughter found the document and was willing to meet me at the junction which would save me eighty miles. Meanwhile the attorney located his copy. The trip was not necessary.

The real estate agent apologized profusely. I said, "Mistakes happen; we all make them. I forgive you totally." The closing agent said, "This is the third deal I have done for you this year, and they have all been less than wonderful. I am afraid to do any more for you." "On the contrary," I said, "I want you to do all my deals. We are used to each other. I do not want to train anyone else on the fine art of crisis management."

God gives us opportunity after opportunity all day long to do things his way. Being a Christian does not mean situations run smoothly for you. It means you are learning to trust God so you can run smoothly through situations.

I know God was with me because I know how my human nature would have handled that situation in the past. By all human standards I had every right to be angry and to call them both on the carpet for incompetence. Acting on self-centered human emotions, we hurt others. I am so grateful for having received God's forgiveness. Passing it on is a privilege. The peace of knowing I followed his direction is priceless.

Christianity is not boring and restrictive. It is challenging and very exciting when we know we are victorious because we did it God's way. Are we always successful? No, but we are always forgiven when we sincerely confess our lapse in commitment. Then we are sent back to try again.

Through all of the upheaval I had clung to the vision of living in my log cabin. Then one morning I asked God for an answer concerning my desire to own the dream house. "What is your will for me in this situation?" The answer was immediate. My response was calm surrender. God took me to a new level of understanding, and it made the difference between my emotional human nature begging him to "make my plan work" and the solid peace that comes with hearing God speak these words:"You are to stay where you are for now. Your family needs you. You have to tie up all the loose ends of your life; it is not time to leave.

CHAPTER SEVEN

GOD'S TIME AND TIMING

Time, We run out of it, try to extend it, organize it, or use it wisely. We waste it, bide it, manipulate it, try to beat it, capture it, and buy it. Time keeps its own pace steadily forward. It is unaffected by any of our perceptions or scattered efforts to restructure it. God's time is not measurable by us. God's timing is not something we could ever manage. He is the only one who controls the whole plan.

One of the amazing results of aligning my life with Christ was immediate, a result I actually felt in my physical body. I had been driving ahead in life like an old steam-engine train racing at full speed. The engine was suddenly stopped. All the car hitches slammed into each other in succession. Once the train was completely stopped, there was silence—then the hissing of pressure released the sense of hesitation to wait for the right timing. Slowly my engine moved ahead, and each hitch clanked into place. Each car jerked into line following in controlled peace. Then I realized I would definitely reach my destination without the breakneck speed. The difference would be the enjoyment, depth of experience, and peace in all I would go through along the way.

I found I was able to accomplish more in a day than ever before, because of my willingness to listen to God's leading. At the end of the day, I was learning to lay before God those things that are not in my hands to change. I concentrated on those issues of life in which I could be effective. The almost unbelievable weight rose from my shoulders. I had more energy functioning in God's time frame. I put my leather-bound organizer into storage. I began to operate on God's instruction. I followed the leading of the Holy Spirit.

During the day I would be working on the computer or doing the laundry, and someone's name would enter my mind. I would drop what I was doing and make a call or send an e-mail. Every time, the contact would result in filling a need for someone else, or for me. It was not always a "trumpets and angels" moment, most of the time it was a mild "aha" moment, followed by "Thank you, God." I learned to look forward to what God had in mind. I kept order when dealing with the maintenance of life, so chores could be put on autopilot. Doing that created an atmosphere that allowed me more time to develop my relationship with Christ. Please understand there were many distractions and much chaos coming at me every day. Learning to live a new life, while dying to the old, is exhausting. I was at once an observer of myself from both sides of the chasm as well as a participant in each life.

I can hear you saying, "But you have no idea what I have to do every day. If I don't keep control, everything and everyone in my world will fly apart." Oh, really? If you die tomorrow, have you trained an apprentice to step in at a moment's notice and carry on your importance? No, time will go on. The people in our sphere of influence will take a week to dispose of our remains. They will scatter our possessions and begin their process of grief. Others will take up the slack and fill or eliminate our self-proclaimed exalted position. We become a memory. All we are in this world is our contribution. The quality of the memory and contribution should be of great importance to us. We have the capacity to really influence others for God by how we reflect his love in his world.

Early in my new relationship, when an eleventh hour was fast approaching, I would clutch in my solar plexus. Old patterns of control would rise up like a snake from a coil. At those times, in my former life, frantic thrashings of "take charge" would begin. The release of adrenaline and panic would take over. I worked frantically to resolve the issue. Exhaustion set in. Nothing of any value took place. No permanent solution was reached. My life was controlled by circumstance.

Now, the chain of command is clear. I can know the eleventh hour is coming but know that God will be there. I excitedly anticipate God's solution. That knowledge makes me more passionate about following Christ and abandoning my old ways. Now, I work each day, each minute, to stay in God's will. I never want to lose my relationship with the creator who made the gift of a renewed life a reality for me.

A very important response from God concerning time and timing happened in November 2007. I had been praying for deliverance from stagnation for my immediate family since the spring of 2007, a steady communication with God, asking for help and relief from painful circumstances. Then in September my prayer changed. I offered God, in prayer, what I was willing to do to effect the change. *"Dear heavenly Father, none of us are moving forward to accomplish your plan in our lives. I will do whatever you ask, even if it means leaving my daughter and grandsons and selling my home. I trust you completely; shake it up as much as it takes, and I will trust your decision and even be excited about it. You are the only one who knows which log to release to move us all forward into the current. I ask this in the name of your beloved son, and our savior Jesus Christ. Thank you, Lord that you hear my prayers and always answer."*

In November I took a vacation, to visit friends. It was the first vacation I had taken in almost ten years. I had a wonderful time. I love to drive, and the weather was so perfect, it had a dreamlike quality to it. I spent time with friends, just enjoying their company, without any of us feeling the pressure of having to entertain each other. Their beautiful home and movie-set patio were a haven of tranquility.

The weather was unusually warm for late fall, and even on the drive home I escaped any hint of winter weather until the last eighty miles of the drive. During my stay, I received an e-mail from my sister who lived with my mother. She, my sister, had been diagnosed with congestive heart failure and had decided to move back to the Midwest to be closer to medical care and her children. She intended to take Mother with her and move into an assisted living facility. I told her I would drive directly to their home when I left and talk about what was happening.

In the beginning it was a magical drive through fascinating desert and majestic high country. The ease of the trip gave me time to think about what I would be facing.

Eighty miles from my destination, in weather that had now turned to winter and darkness, a deer committed suicide on the hood of my car. He ran full bore into the right front fender. As I stood on the brakes and hung myself on the seatbelt he came down on the hood. He shot off into the opposite lane of traffic and was run over by three more cars. The fourth car was driven by a highway patrolman, who turned around to assist me. By this time I had pulled off to the side of the road, shaken, trying to make sense of what had happened. He took all the appropriate steps of questioning, comforting, and filling out forms. Then he said "I can't let you continue on because you have no headlights. You will have to go back to town and get a room."

Before receiving my sister's e-mail, I had gone shopping in Arizona for supplies for the winter. I had a van filled to the roof line, including my heavy oxygen concentrator and breathing equipment, none of which could be left in a car on a freezing night. I drove into town with pieces of my car dropping on the road every few feet. I found a motel, unloaded everything into my room, and traversed the ice-covered parking lot to get dinner-to-go. Once back in my room I phoned all interested family members to tell them the news, took a shower, and went to bed. I knew what was coming would be life changing. God had heard me. The next day I rallied, repacked the car, and found a body shop. I unpacked the car into a rental car, signed appropriate paperwork, and by two o'clock was on the last leg of my trip. I arrived in a snowstorm, exhausted, and in a fair amount of pain. From that point, life took on a surreal and whirlwind form.

I had asked God in prayer for his plan and committed to do whatever he wanted me to do. After I had visited with my mother and sister, God clearly spoke to my heart. I knew he wanted me to take over the care of my mother. The reason I knew he spoke to me? When I heard him, I surrendered to his will and was peaceful about the answer ... no regrets and no doubts. The next day I asked my mother, "If you could make a choice, would you choose to move? I need you to give me a straight, honest answer." She said, "No, I don't want to move. It is too much work and too much of an adjustment to start over at ninety-three years old." I said "Then how about my moving up here with you?" To which she answered, "I would love it, but what about your kids?" I told her they would understand, and we would all survive the change.

Now, when you pray as a committed Christian, you must be ready to accept all that God requires. This is what I had prayed for, so there was no way I could or would disobey. The peace that comes when you are where God wants you is unmistakable. The joy carried me to a level of excitement over this new direction. I knew I would never live in my house again.

From November 14, 2007, to January 14, 2008, was a period of intensity that challenged every aspect of my old personality. Wyoming was having the hardest winter in many years. I had to live with the summer clothes I had brought from warmer country. No coat and my gloves were in my car, which had sustained $7,000 worth of damage and was eighty miles away. It took until the week before Christmas to be repaired. Meanwhile, the days flew by as I arranged for a place for my sister to live, while she packed up her life. I coordinated the moving van with the destination and traveled through snow and ice several times for doctor appointments for my mother and sister. It was ninety miles one way in an unfamiliar rented car. We were told after we arrived for one appointment that the x-ray machine was broken and they would call when it was repaired. There was dealing with paperwork for all that was going on, arranging for therapy for my mother in a house that was turned upside down with moving, cleaning out and rearranging the house, along with all the daily chores.

At the same time I was trying to deal with my own bills and business, with all my records and computer at home. Every night after I fixed dinner, I returned to where I was staying at my brother-in-law's. I spent a couple of hours in prayer and conversation with God. I never complained about God's plan. I knew this was the answer to my prayer. I would be given the strength to complete the project, and this was where I needed to be, to be in God's will. I also spent many nights in tears at the thought of leaving my daughter and grandsons. Each day I resolved to handle every issue with patience and a pleasant attitude. I did not always live up to that goal. The important thing is that I did not give in to how "old self" would have responded. Each day, God gave me everything I needed to do the job. I kept my inner peace.

I had to make a trip to my home in southern Wyoming to get my bed, winter clothes, computer, and anything else I could fit in the car. The stress was unbelievable, but there was more to come. My brother-in-law drove me to the town, eighty miles away, to get my car the week before Christmas. I continued on and spent a few days at home, visiting my family, and packing up my belongings. Then I left under blue skies to head back north. The weather was deceiving. Forty miles down the road, I hit intermittent ground blizzards, and by the time I entered the freeway, it was too late to turn back. I was committed to a twenty-mile drive to a major city in blizzard conditions that forced the left lane traffic to ride the center line and the right lane traffic to drive within six inches of the center line. I have never been that close to big rigs. The rivets on the sides of the trucks were all I could see out my side window. The exit to the city was barely recognizable. It was impossible to go on, so I headed for the motel and stood thirty-fifth in line to get a room.

The freeway had been closed, and hundreds of people were stranded. Finally I secured a room and proceeded to unload my car. There was no elevator, and my room was on the second floor, with an outside entrance halfway down the balcony that no one had had time to shovel. The wind blew seventy miles an hour all night, creating snowdrifts with the density of concrete.

Three members of a Colorado family were killed that afternoon west of town on the freeway. They were on their way to celebrate the holidays on the coast. The lone surviving daughter was airlifted to a trauma center. That news put everything in perspective, and I thanked God for getting me safely to shelter unharmed. I prayed for the child who had lost her whole family. Two days later, I was back on the freshly plowed roads, and it appeared the weather would be clear. The skies were blue, and the sun was out. Fifty miles into the trip on a desolate highway, severe ground blizzards lay in wait. Grateful for being alone on the highway I crawled along from marker to marker, straining to see, for the next eighty miles. At one point I passed a truck that had blown over into the ditch on its top. The highway patrol and wrecker were with the driver. Gaining a better grip on the wheel I approached the rim of the canyon and started down thirty miles of 7 percent grade into the next town. The only comfort was knowing the patrol car and wrecker would be coming behind me. I drove twenty miles an hour, with the wind driving a steady horizontal wall of snow into the side of my van. Had it not been for the full load in the back, I would have been the next customer for the wrecker. An hour later the patrolman caught up, and instead of passing, me he stayed behind me for the last ten miles into town.

I was exhausted from the strain of the trip and still had eighty miles to go. The weather improved and left only the ice-rutted road to contend with for the next forty miles, then dry roads to home. The car was unloaded and things put away, but I could not sit down even for a minute. I had promised to cook Christmas dinner for ten and headed over to my brother-in-law's to prepare the meal ahead of time to ease the work the next day. It was my first Christmas without my daughter and grandchildren, and it was good to celebrate with a group. The bad weather increased. After Christmas we settled in to finish all the details of my sister's move.

The movers were a week late due to weather and finally arrived to make short work of unloading the house. On January 14, we drove 200 miles to the nearest airport in wind and snow on icy roads. We stayed in a motel that night, so my sister would not miss her flight in the morning. The motel took our reservations over the phone without letting us know they were under construction. The in-house restaurants were closed. Negotiating two physically challenged people in seventy-mile-an-hour winds out to a restaurant in the dark is no easy task. The next day the wind was a steady fifty miles an hour, with gusts of seventy when we left the motel. Once my sister's plane took off, Mother and I drove home through bad weather on a hundred-mile stretch of road that does not even have a rest area, let alone a town, and were very grateful to God for our once again safe return.

Then, we began our new life together. Mom was beginning to feel better, due to the steps taken to improve her medical conditions. Macular degeneration had progressed to the point where she could no longer sew, quilt, or read. God led me to a service for the visually impaired. They provided a machine which allowed her to put reading material under a magnifying camera which transfers it to a computer screen enabling her to read. The same service provided her with an audio book system.

Snow and outrageous windstorms kept me from making another trip to my house until April, to tie up loose ends and bring back more things. Again God's timing was better. On April 9, 2008, Mother and I headed for South Dakota, to meet my third sister and transfer Mother to her care for a two-week visit. I went to my home to work for two weeks, putting my possessions either in the storage shed or in my car. I visited with friends and had a little repair work done on the house. My daughter also reevaluated what she had, repacking boxes and storing them in an extra shed I had on my property. She weeded out and donated boxes to the thrift shop. It was a productive two weeks and fit perfectly into God's later plan. Then it was time to return to Wall, South Dakota, to pick up my mother and return to her home with a van full of my life. It took me a week to unload the car and filter my things into an already full house.

I did not want to sell my house right away because I had not had much time to sit down and think about how and when to do it. I prayed for God's will to be accomplished and for me to hear and understand how I was to dispose of the property. When I could catch my breath, I remembered my prayers almost a year earlier. God had given me everything I had asked him for, but in his way, the last thing was the selling of my house. Three weeks later, instead of waiting for a word from God, I was influenced by the secular world, which indicated that I must put the house on the market during the selling season, and it all made sense to me. I took steps immediately. I called the real estate agent and listed the house. The agent called me two days later to tell me two more houses had just been listed at the same price, so there would be more competition than expected. I had no qualms, because I knew that my house would eventually sell. I would receive exactly what God wanted me to have from the sale.

In the middle of May I again headed for home to prepare the house for sale. If I had waited to hear from God about when to sell the house, my daughter would have had time to make the decision to ask if she could take over the costs of the house and move herself and my grandsons into it. Because I rushed out ahead of God, I had to stand the cost of maintaining an empty house for six months. She called and asked me not to relist it, saying that she wanted to move in and take over the bills. It was a perfect solution for me, for her, and for the house. This is what is meant by listening for God's plan. When God through Jesus Christ is in control of events in your life, you just do not have to worry—if you pray and listen for his perfect timing.

Follow his lead and obey his commands no matter what you or the world may think. It does not mean you sit back on your rocker and do nothing. You will work harder and longer than you ever have or thought you could. You can, because you are given strength to complete any task God gives you.

I am writing this book, caring for my ninety-four-year- old mother, moving, and dealing with my own fairly debilitating health issues. I also work part time on my computer. I maintain a home and do all the shopping, cooking, and cleaning. I am also responsible for all the financial and medical paperwork for me, my mother, and my husband. He is staying with his daughter in another state to receive the medical care he needs. I tell you this not to brag but to say I could not do this without God and the strength, peace, time, timing, and direction he gives me on a daily basis. The only delays or bumps in my road are the ones I create.

My life was now turned in a new direction, and it was time to address some issues of discipline concerning my health and less than perfect body. At such a turning point, you must first take stock of the reality of the remodeling job ahead. It does not matter what food plan you undertake, which twenty-dollar-a-month state-of-the-art exercise and torture machine you purchase to use as a clothes rack, or whether you run every morning until your lungs bleed. You will never develop perfectly formed legs, breasts like cantaloupes, or a long torso which includes a waist, if you did not start out with that framework. Diet and exercise will not grow parts that were nonexistent when you began your restoration.

In my case, I was over sixty, and my frame looked as if I had been placed in a trash compactor at birth. Picture a penguin with blue eyes and straight graying hair. Add a bottom rib which collides with my hip bone if I do one of those side-stretch exercise moves. You know the one where the willowy blond Amazon next to you in class creates a perfect curve from armpit to the top of her thigh when she makes the same move. My body is crisscrossed with stretch marks from pregnancy and scars from surgeries. They would only sag and wrinkle with the loss of the fat that is keeping them smooth at this point. No amount of cocoa butter is going to cure that problem.

Make sure your expectations for the overhaul equal your own reality. Remember, we are all one-of-a-kind creations. We owe it to God to take the best care of ourselves we can. To accomplish that takes effort, commitment, and desire. None of us have all those things running at 100 percent capacity all the time. God understands that, even when your personal trainer, dietitian, and the critical eyes waiting for you to fail do not understand. Press on.

After completing the reality check and asking God for his help in undoing all the physical havoc I had wreaked on my body, I promised to begin to love all of myself and bring the body out of mothballs to be put in service for him. He had given me the time and structure I needed and then put me in a location that has exercise equipment in the local senior center. There is also a brand-new fitness center with state-of-the-art equipment at an affordable monthly rate for seniors. There may or may not be a loving relationship with the fitness center. Routine exercise has never been a dream of mine. God does have a way of removing excuses from our path to allow us to succeed—even if we would prefer he whack us with a wand and remove all our problems. I have neatly avoided going to the fitness center, with one excuse or another, but maybe I will go look at it one of these days.

Where will we be spending eternity? That is the decision we must make before we die. Who are we when we are stripped of our self-created importance? When all our sins of choice, treasures, achievements, and circles of familiarity and control are gone? What is left? Take the time in this life to become intimate and familiar with your future. Preparation is the purpose of life. The only real choice is to decide which eternal life we wish to prepare for. There is nothing wrong with achievements, treasures, and position if they are of God. Without salvation and serving God with all the gifts he gave us, we totally miss our life's purpose. Difficult and painful events still happen. Handling them with Father, Son, and Holy Spirit makes us effective in what God asks us to do. It teaches us to trust the rest to God and his time and timing.

CHAPTER EIGHT

CHANGES IN THE TEMPLE

There are many changes happening now, in my soul, spirit, and my body, which is referred to in the Bible as a temple. My body is more like Angkor Wat being consumed by jungle than the radiant Taj Mahal. Some changes are subtle, some overt, but all fall in stages of upward progression.

I had researched for years the mysterious maladies that plague my body. Over the years I have been diagnosed with faulty metabolism, multiple sclerosis, lupus, and at last fibromyalgia. I also battle candida and thyroid problems. I have injuries to joints and flesh that limit my ability to exercise on a regular basis, even if I were a devotee.

Food, Friendly and Demonic

I had completely changed the contents of the food cupboards and the refrigerator, in 2006, to match a popular alternative health expert's plan for healthy living. However, I think most of you can relate to adding the occasional dish of ice cream or bowl of popcorn to your diet. And don't forget the inspiration to design your own pizza from the gourmet deli. I finally had to come to terms with the fact that I was not normal and could not have sugar or carbohydrates, unless they were shaped like vegetables and fruits, and that I must also shun any foods that have mold or yeast content. If I choose to eat them, the consequence will be weight gain. Although the information was valuable, I could not stay on the plan. The plan called for too much protein and fat, and my kidneys began to throw stones again. I have suffered for years with serious joint pain, swollen legs, numb feet, numb lower legs, brain fog, and a myriad of other enervating demons. The radiation treatments from my bout with cancer took their toll, as did all the operations and quarts of antibiotics pumped into my system during each and every operation. And a special thanks to all the excessive x-rays and MRIs over the years.

The emotional issues surrounding comfort food were difficult to control also. I prayed about it many times but never totally followed the instructions given to me. I have always been a problem solver. The guilt of not being able to solve or manage issues with my own body was too difficult for me to accept. I mentally separated my soul and self from my physical body. I referred to it as the "uncooperative thing"— not repairable, and unable to keep up with me. So I left it behind. I washed it, clothed it, maintained it, and took it in for medical treatment when necessary. I lost much of it to major surgeries and cancer. I never admitted to a personal relationship with it.

Only after my rebirth did I begin to integrate my mental, spiritual, and physical self, really taking an interest in caring for all of me—right down to the need for the dreaded exercise program. I freely admit that my attitude about exercise has been less than enthusiastic. I was a firm believer in hard physical work, adamant in the belief that exhaustion, sore muscles, and aching joints should produce a well-manicured lawn or a clean, organized room. I was so disconnected from my body that I did not understand that the end result of the proper diet and exercise and energy output could be a healthy body. I just did not have any interest in an organized, disciplined exercise routine. I could not visualize the end result. The strange thing is I am far from being a couch potato. I am not undisciplined, except for exercise, nor do I have an uncontrollable appetite. I had quit smoking cold turkey for fifteen years and started up again for five years. I quit again cold turkey at age fifty-one, in the middle of my bout with cancer, when my grandson's birth was imminent. I was determined to have a smoke-free environment in which he could visit Grandma. Eventually, through restructuring my foods and taking high-quality vitamins and supplements, I managed to bring all my blood test results into the proper ranges. I was the healthiest overweight person the medical people had seen. I have yet to crack the code for the actual losing of pounds. I suspect it has something to do with the aforementioned and despicable "exercise regimen."

On May 1, 2008, I surrendered it all in prayer to God, through Jesus Christ. *"Dear heavenly Father, show me my path to the good health and strength I will need to do your will. I cannot take the pain anymore and will need all the energy I can muster to do whatever you ask of me. Even though I have made sincere efforts, my stubborn will wants to have the kinds of food that poison my system. I need your help to overcome the self-pity I feel when I can't eat like others. I need to break the emotional and social cravings tied to food and stop using weight as a barrier to protect myself from emotional pain. Thank you, God, for listening to, hearing, and answering all my prayers in the name of your precious Son, Jesus Christ."*

Two days went by. Then I began a one-week trip through a valley of serious brain fog, joint pain, and aching in my flesh reminiscent of the Asian flu. On the ninth of May I reached critical mass and could not take the misery any longer. I was ready to accept the fact that I could not eat sugar or carbs other than the kind found in vegetables. I had suffered all day and was at an incredible low. I had asked God to deliver me from this problem, and his reply was "I will help you deliver yourself from the problem."

Body Shop

May 9, 2008, was my day to begin the body restoration. That night my back ached and my flesh hurt all over. I had made another decision not to take any ibuprofen or any of the other pain medication prescribed to me. Shooting pains were going everywhere. I finally got to sleep but woke up several times from the pain. I decided God clearly wanted me to be acutely aware of what had hold of me. Even though I had changed the kitchen over to meet the food plan, I still continued to play with it, still trying to have what I wanted and diet. I wanted to be normal. I had to face the fact that I was not. I was still just maintaining my weight. It would vary one to ten pounds daily depending on whether or not I took my water pill. My hair was very dry, and I itched all over. I would experience what can only be described as bugs biting me everywhere. There was pain in my joints, flesh, and muscles, serious inflammation that made me want to scream. I was exhausted from fighting pain. My feet had been numb for years on the surface. The fluid buildup in my legs and feet was so painful and debilitating that I could not bend my feet or ankles. I made an appointment with the doctor to see if my thyroid medication was correct. After testing, he decided it should be increased in strength.

During one of my sleepless spells that night, God instructed me to fast for three days. I was to take an antifungal for the systemic candida and begin eating fruit and vegetables in earnest. On the morning of May10, 2008, I took my medications and supplements with a four-ounce glass of orange juice. I stirred a healthy dose of antifungal in some juice and downed it with my vitamins. I drank only water for the rest of the day and the next two days. At the end of the fast I was already beginning to feel better. The problem had been the addition of self-prescribed treats and then the yeast escalated. I was feeding the fungus the sugar it wanted, and fungus is never satisfied. My back pain was greatly reduced, and it took less time to fall asleep. I'd had a serious bout with one of my periodic fits of brain fog the day before I started the fast. I have always been in pain in my joints and flesh, in varying degrees. I only discovered what normal pain-free life was during one of my too many surgeries. I was given morphine and woke up to a pain-free world.

From May 11, 2008, to the first part of July, I struggled to stay on the plan. As good as it is there was a missing component for my individual makeup. I could not keep my blood sugar level and was still napping and having energy spikes and crashes. I was losing weight but slowly. I had the hot buttered popcorn affair under control, but ice cream was another story, and I still wanted to have those occasional social events with friends and eat like everyone else. Human will is stronger than glue.

Then I took a necessary short trip. As all you dieters-in-perpetuity know, calories consumed outside a fifty-mile radius of your home, while you are traveling, do not add pounds. You factor in a land speed of sixty-five miles an hour, and of course you outrun them. I have other examples of convoluted logic, but this will give you the reason I gained back five of the lost pounds. As I drove into the outer rim of the fifty-mile radius of home, I was once again at the feet of Jesus stating my resolve.

On July 15 the starting gun fired again, and I began to lose. I made the statement that I would not veer from the plan even if company came. They could eat what I cooked or find a restaurant. That's right, company came. I did succumb to flesh, but beyond a couple of indiscretions, all went well, and only three pounds were regained. They left in short order. And again I pledged my resolve.

This battle against years of pattern, habit, and comfort foods is a monumental struggle. It cannot be cured with the latest marketing miracle or surgery. In the end it is always personal discipline with God's help. You have to have help that does not condemn or leave you feeling like a failure. It will also not be solved wallowing in hours of introspection. Take a quick look at the food you love and follow it back to a point of connection with feeling loved and secure. For example, as mentioned earlier, I have had since childhood an addiction to old-fashioned regular popcorn with just the right amount of butter. It was the main comfort food in my life—Sunday night popcorn and apple suppers with all of us around the table or sitting in the living room laughing and talking, sometimes a fire in the fireplace, warm, safe, and loved.

We are not talking about a normal consumer, but a person who made certain the shelf was stocked with popcorn at all times. Through all the stresses of my life after leaving home, the first thing I thought of to relieve the stress was a bowl of popcorn. When the change of eating habits became important to me, I stopped eating popcorn addictively, though. I refused to give it up altogether. I asked God in prayer for help in breaking my addiction to popcorn.

Then one day in September 2008, after four days fighting a craving for popcorn, I bought some and made a batch for Sunday night dinner.

I became very ill that night. The popcorn sat at the top of my stomach like a blob of rising bread dough. I was up most of the night with bouts of nausea, and the very sight of the leftovers in the popcorn bowl sent my stomach into barrel rolls. It lasted three weeks, and even writing about it brings back the nausea.

My family was dumbstruck, because my reputation as consummate popcorn gourmet was legendary. I had heard over the years about alcoholics and drug addicts coming to Christ asking to be released from their addiction and then instantly putting down their drug of choice, never touching it again, or at least having limited the intake. I did not believe it was possible. Now I indulge in popcorn once in a while, but it does not have control over me. I now put regular popcorn in brown paper bags, which I tape shut and microwave, and instead of butter I use olive oil.

We can go back to God for more instruction and insight. God helps us rely on him, as we said we would do when we accepted salvation. His love will lift us through the process. We have to do the hard work of undoing all the destruction we cause in our bodies by following our sinful human nature, and we must accept responsibility for the results. Now I can, with God's help, make friends with this body. I will continue on with fruits and vegetables until a better plan is brought to my attention. It may take longer than it does on a half-hour sitcom, but it will happen. Not that I won't succumb to a treat now and then. I will enjoy it and get right back on track. It took years to store up these calories, and they will have to come off in a slow and steady process, while I am taking on other assignments. I did start using the exercise machines at the senior center; consistency is still a problem, but I am working on the issue.

I mentioned my attitude toward people in general in an earlier chapter, a result of my "mirror, mirror" image of myself. Slowly, through this process of rebirth, I have noticed a willingness and even an enthusiasm on my part to join groups of people just for the pleasure of their company and to engage strangers in conversation to learn about them. I am looking for ways to serve and to help but not with the same motivation as before. I now ask God to direct me in the way he would have me help or serve.

Serving without concern about where it will lead us or how it will make us feel or calculating whether or not it is important is a joyous experience. We ask God what he wants of us, we obey, and it pleases God. Because of our obedience, God takes care of our needs in ways we never could have imagined. Taking our place in God's family through rebirth makes it clear we are different from each other only because of circumstances in our lives. We are not better or worse than each other in God's eyes. We set ourselves apart from each other by setting up human lines of demarcation. We use money, physical appearance, lineage, IQ, etc., to draw the lines. In God's eyes we are all of equal value. Competition is a human standard for measuring value.

SUBMISSION

I have always had a difficult time with the word of God concerning submission. Here I stand at this time in my life, with one divorce and a second failed marriage with no divorce. Both marriage commitments were made without the original architect of marriage having been consulted or made a partner. It never mattered to me who wanted to marry whom, because I saw marriage more as a legal necessity. Now I know marriage is a three-way partnership. Both people need to come to a true marriage having established their own relationship with God. Then they have the strength and the structure that allows two strangers to build a life and family as God intended. I believe marriage is God's plan for the formation and structure of a family which includes procreation—an impossible task for same-sex couples. It is a biblical contract between God, a man, and a woman for procreation and the establishment of the family unit. It is also recorded as a legal contract. There are other legal avenues for unions outside of the one God gave the world. Marriage has been clearly defined as God's covenant. It should not be hijacked in an attempt to sanctify other types of relationships. I find it very curious that same-sex couples, who protest traditional conservative values based on the Bible, want so desperately to "be married." It would make more sense if they wanted to be as far removed from marriage as possible.

I personally no longer have the desire to be yoked to anyone else in this life. I am peaceful, joyous and energized in my single life. I look forward to new assignments from God. That does not mean I do not believe, particularly as a single parent, in the importance of a Christ-centered marriage and a male and female parenting team.

Boxes of Ego and Distraction, Neatly Stacked

In my former life, before Christ, I spent exhaustive hours stacking the boxes of distractive ego- driven projects into controlled and organized configurations. After I had accepted Christ, God began to kick the boxes out from under me and scatter them so far that they were irretrievable. One by one, in every area of my life God removed my self-importance—that is, those things which kept me "busy" and looking important. Busy work kept me from looking at more parts of me that needed cleaning. I was making every effort to follow God's leading daily, but the time came to look at deeper issues. And those things I thought defined me he stripped away. My sins were forgiven, past, present, and future. Now it was time to learn about commitment, to understand and eliminate the chaff in my life.

As mentioned earlier, I had held a seat on a county board for twelve years, chairing the board for three terms. A considerable amount of time was spent on the work it took to plan and execute the responsibilities of the board. I relied on the administrative assistant for some of the responsibility and trusted in her abilities. She was also a member of the same church I attended. She turned out to be a prime example of a shark in a dolphin suit.

It soon became clear her agenda was to force me and a fellow employee off the board. She considered us a threat to her grab for power. I confronted the board with what was happening. I fully expected support from the people I had worked with for so long. I was wrong and found myself up against an evil for which I was not prepared. I resigned from the board. Although the experience hurt me deeply, it was probably the only way I would have left the position. The position fed my ego, even though it clearly had served its purpose in my life. The board realized about a year later the brand of evil they had regrettably backed.

Selling online was something I began doing in 1998 to turn our possessions into cash. It turned into a steady cash flow and remained an ongoing garage sale experience for a number of years. I began to sell for others on a commission basis. The online selling company was a simple system when it began, but like many good ideas it grew beyond efficient simplicity and affordability. In the end, it was too unwieldy, complicated, and expensive to make sense to the individual seller.

I pressed on stubbornly, using precious time to keep the now diminishing cash flow coming, spending time away from writing the book. One day I sat down to list some items on the website. I found there was a new rule requiring sellers to use a third-party pay system for my customers. If I did not offer this system to buyers, I could no longer sell with the online company. Again, I would not have stopped on my own; something had to stop me. God had to pull the support out of my life to increase my reliance on him to provide what was necessary in my life.

With the elimination of those two activities, I gained about eight hours a day. I was able to throw away several boxes of paperwork and files. The clearing out and ridding myself of old projects and dead-end dreams continued in earnest. I cleared out books, purged more files, divested my life of clothes that did not fit, gave away gadgets and duplicates of any of those objects that might come in handy sometime. Then Satan ramped up his attacks. Over the course of a few months he threw many distractions at me. He succeeded in drawing me back into empty endeavors—my involvement in a number of community committee projects and a major legal fight against the US Forest Service. Those had to go also. But one of them lingered for a while and led to another major upheaval lasting eighty-six days from start to finish.

In the summer of 2006 I offered the use of my property to house a farmers' market. It had formerly been located in an obscure part of town with minimum exposure. The vendors had also been harassed by the local retailers and came to me asking for a new location. The moving of the farmers' market brought a barrage of hateful acts from the townspeople. The vendors said they had never experienced such miserable treatment in any town on the circuit.

At the same time the friend who had supported me through the church discipline issue in an earlier chapter wanted to partner with me to build a restaurant on my property. She started with a wonderful little sandwich wagon. She hired a friend of hers to run it, and we began the legal work of setting up a corporation. We drew plans and tried to work with the town to correct a water line problem they had created. She hired an engineering firm to develop a water and sewer plan.

The sandwich shop belonged to my friend, and I kept the books. We stored all the food and supplies in my house and hosted the farmers' market. My house became sandwich production central. In the middle of it all our pastor's wife and three others of us held a Bible study one day a week. All the plates begin to spin, and the energy and excitement of making something happen reverberated in my flesh. The book was set aside because all this "importance" had to take center stage. Then, right on schedule, it all began to unravel again.

What had started out as a wonderful concept of bringing something good into the community was dashed. What looked like a God-inspired idea belonged again to the enemy. This time the lessons were someone else's. I was watching the very same thing happen to my partner that had happened to me with the child-care project. The friend she hired was using her for personal gain. We received no cooperation from the town with regard to correcting their problem with the water system. Once again the jealousy, negativity, and "no change" attitude of townspeople worked to destroy the plan.

During this time, someone else asked me to help form a recreational organization in the valley. The idea was worthy, and I had some skills that could contribute to its success. Again it was empty effort, and many more hours of my life were spent in using my talents and skills to accomplish nothing. Finally I got it through my head that the seventeen years I had spent in trying to improve the community was totally wasted. My time, talents, and heart were to go in God's direction. We humans have such a difficult time staying on task. God has endless patience.

I stopped doing everything and returned total focus to new life in Christ. No matter how cataclysmic the salvation experience, it is a constant vigil to keep your choices on track. Distractions and temptations abound in this world. They tend to intensify in strength to come against our commitment. Things really do get worse before they get better. Once again, I pulled out the book material and started writing.

Tithing Is Not A Ponzi Scheme

Tithing was never part of my former life. It did not make sense to give away 10 percent of what I had when there were bills to pay. Here again, I asked God for everything. I never considered he wanted me to give something back besides my claim that I loved him. Finally I understood that everything belongs to God. All he is asking for is a 10 percent return to go into the furthering of his kingdom to show our love and commitment to him. I began to give, even when I had very little. My first tithe was the last two dollars in my wallet. I mailed it to the church anonymously. I gave and trusted God to take care of my needs. He did. I received a check in the mail in the form of a refund of overpayment that I did not know about. God wants us to do what he asks of us, no matter how impossible it looks to us, and trust him for "how it will happen." Let go of the controls and watch him work through you.

By all human understanding I should have lost everything and been out on the street with all that had happened. God, though, has made a way ever since I turned it all over to him. The mortgage on my house was reduced by $550 a month. It happened through an amazing set of circumstances that put it into the hands of a private lender. The terms were extremely generous, with an interest rate that turned out to match today's lending rates. Without that turn of events, I would have lost my house in the current state of the economy.

Someone anonymously paid for the bulk of my propane for one winter season. People came in and out of my life at pivotal moments. They delivered information, money, goods, services, time, and friendship, all of which kept me going. They were all gifts from God. I made a point of passing gifts forward whenever a need arose that God asked me to meet.

I look back in amazement at what God has done in my life for the last five years, without my deserving it or earning it. When something went wrong in my previous life, I would mockingly sing, "Jesus doesn't love me, this I know, for this problem tells me so," when all the time he loved me more than any human being has the ability to do. Now he has forgiven me all my insulting behavior toward him. I do not have to be dragged down in shame for the rest of my life. Why do we humans resist being completely loved and forgiven?, because we are rebellious by nature.

Abortion Is The Taking Of Life

My position on and understanding of abortion changed dramatically after my rebirth. I now know life begins when God infuses spirit into the physical union of egg and sperm. Conception is the union of body, spirit, and love, a Trinity. God creates life in that moment. The definition of life has to be when God joins spirit with human cells; physical death, when the soul leaves human form, because the soul never dies. It enters the body and leaves the body whole and complete. Taking a life through abortion is the same as any other form of taking a life. Anyone who promotes or participates in this horrific, murderous act will be held accountable to God. But even for this act of murder and other vile outcomes of human nature, there is forgiveness and peace waiting through true repentance and salvation.

There are millions of women who were convinced over thirty years ago that part of their right to freedom included choosing between going through with a pregnancy and choosing to terminate it for any reason. They were fed baseless verbal opiates by false teachers. They were convinced the child in their womb was a blob of cells, an unfeeling, unresponsive, expendable nonperson. A case cannot be made for murder by ignoring facts and declaring the victim a nonhuman. I am not talking about those cases of rape, incest, or medical reasons that involve the health of the mother. Those are serious case-by-case decisions to be made by parent or parents, along with spiritual and medical advisers. However, those choices do not change the fact that a life will be taken. Eternal consequences will follow those choices, without sincere repentance.

I am talking about the millions of women who considered legalized abortion to be a form of birth control, the doctors who charge enormous fees to perform the abortions, and the organizations whose purpose is to brainwash women and girls about the act of abortion. We are talking about more lives disposed of than Hitler dispensed with in his career. Where do we call a halt to pro-choice, if not at conception? Countless women who made the choice to terminate their babies' lives are suffering emotionally to this day. Where were the advocates of pro-choice when it came to a choice of birth control methods or the choice of responsible living and self-respect over selfish need and desire? In no other human relationship are we allowed to kill another person without punishment just because we do not want to go through with our commitment to a relationship.

It is not our job to punish and kill abortionists and their victim patients. Christ does not call us to threaten and frighten women entering abortion clinics or to blow up the clinics and murder the doctors. We are called to do battle in a manner that creates a desire for people to follow Christ. God will bring justice to all. He will also forgive those who truly turn to him for salvation. It is our job to reach out to the mothers and fathers and bring them to Christ through compassionate actions in support of them as people in need of our love and help. We need to set up pro-life clinics near the abortion clinics. We can then offer God's answer to these struggling mothers. Finally, it is our responsibility to instill the love of God so firmly in our children that they have respect and love for themselves and life in all forms. If we humans have no respect for life at conception, it follows we will have no basis for respecting life at any level.

We come from Creator God with his divinely intended purpose of serving him on his earth. We are to use the specific gifts and talents he gives us at conception in preparation for our return to him. One gift he gives equally is the gift of free will. With that gift comes one crucial choice: eternal life either with him or without him. You can give your life to Christ and spend your gift of life serving him and trusting him to fulfill his plan for your life. This choice comes with unfailing love and support, as well as unlimited consultation, communication, continuing education, and a guaranteed future in

God's presence. Never being deserted or destroyed in your mistakes, always having sincere repentance as the way back from your human choices. Having the ability, through Christ, to face events which tear at life, with a steady core of joy and trust. Or you can give your life to this world. Follow your human nature, depending on emotional highs and lows, greed, and self-centered motives. Dodging human bullets, who have problems of their own and will only give limited time to yours. Striving to fill your life with things and experiences that will "make you happy," discovering that the "happy" does not last or fill the emptiness inside. Then when you die, you leave it all behind, moving on to endless darkness and separation from God. God gave us the map, compass, example, and explicit directions for a safe return to Him. We must choose to return. We can never return on a path of our own or according to another self-appointed deity's design or choosing. God never rejects us. We make a choice to reject him. He then must judge, as he said he would. Trials in this world are designed to turn us, through Jesus, to God. As new creatures in Christ, we are given a second chance to fulfill our life of service to God.

My mother and I settled into a routine that worked for both of us. Each day I thanked God for the peace in my life and for the privilege of spending time with my mother. She is not perfect, but how could I not forgive her, when I am also an imperfect mother? Life is filled with new friends, not perfect friends. We live in a caring community with a generally pervasive spirit of cooperation. This new life affords me the opportunity to pursue my writing—I am working on my book four to six hours a day—and many opportunities to serve. I am looking for a group of like-minded Christians based in God's word and work. I thank God many times a day for deliverance from myself.

At the end of chapter 7 I mentioned the close and convenient location of a state-of-the-art fitness center. I have driven by it five times. As of December 2008 I had not yet entered the doors to even look around. In the meantime, the fitness center had added the only physical therapist in town, and he accepts Medicare patients. I had just qualified for Medicare at the first of December 2008.

I had been working with a specialist concerning an ongoing physical problem. Then two days before Christmas, I picked up a stapler to staple two sheets of paper together. I snapped something in the wrist of my right hand. The doctor put on a cast and ordered therapy with the new therapist at the fitness center. After three treatments with him, the specialist called with the results of tests. I had fibromyalgia. Part of the treatment is a good exercise program. I then began my therapy treatments for fibromyalgia. After five sessions, the therapist introduced me to the intimidating machinery of exercise equipment. This led to the beginning of a life of discipline and healing. The therapist has become a friend and fantastic support for me. Gently but firmly God began opening doors and pointing the way to what he expected of me.

I would not have chosen fibromyalgia, but I am grateful to a nurse practitioner who took the time to listen to me. She sent me to a doctor who connected the dots. Having an answer frees me from having to do research, looking for answers. Now I can address a real issue, and with God's help I will manage this bump in the road as I move on to other interests. As I grow in Christ, the day will come when I can step away from the condition of fibromyalgia. This new chapter of my life now includes the regular exercise program I was so afraid of. Keep your eyes open in your own life for the "gentle persuasion" of God whenever you try to make an end run around his plan.

CHAPTER NINE

GOD'S PREVENTIVE HEALTHCARE PLAN

Through our relationship with Christ, we are given the power to break addictions and habits. We can end relationships and their destructive influence by forgiving, even if the offending parent, sibling, friend, or stranger is dead by the time we come to Christ. Do not strangle the life out of yourself by saying, "But I can't forgive. You don't know what happened to me." Almost all of us know what the rest of us have been through. We humans share the frailties of our humanity. Forgiveness is for us. We cannot heal without forgiving offense of any kind and turning the offender over to God. However, we must be ready to stop feeding on the carrion of offense.

Forgiveness

Forgiveness is one of the first things God will have us do to deal with the past. It does not end there. Forgiveness must become our automatic response to any future offense. It must become a daily exercise in our lives. Forgiveness of ourselves and forgiveness of others is paramount to good health. Once we accept God's forgiveness and know the wonderful difference it makes in us, we want to forgive and move past the issues.

It's like the difference between an arrow glancing off your shield and one sinking deeply into your flesh. Some of us are even willing to break off the shaft and allow the wound to fester and infect our entire body, rather than pulling it out and letting the wound heal.

Our human nature, working out of our own baggage and following our feelings, takes offense. It returns worse behavior until a standoff is reached. Both parties retreat to lick their wounds and actively seek a group of supporters. Then each party proceeds to extend the fight by talking about it with their friends, often dragging it up with them and linking it to the next offense. Division between camps causes more hard feelings. Soon, no one is speaking to anyone else, no conclusion is in sight, and many are suffering. This cycle never ends, because human nature has no place to lie anything permanently to rest, no real resolution process. The pain remains.

Ask God for the right words or actions to reflect his love, while forgiving the offender. Acting in love will leave you with no time or desire for self-pity or wounded ego. We tap into God's power through our faith in Christ. Our reaction to the offender can be God working through us. Christ's way leaves both parties whole. Those who forgive retain peace, joy, and confidence, knowing they have obeyed and forgiven. The recipients have been offered Christ's love and forgiveness. Now those who have offended have the responsibility of choosing how they will respond. In this scenario only the persons who drew first blood have to deal with the incident. They may continue to live in anger or begin to investigate a life in Christ. Either way, it is their choice. Most important, their poison has not spread.

We find the strength to forgive through our relationship with Christ. Go directly to him through prayer, and ask him to help you forgive an offender. We humans do not give up our wounds easily. They anchor us to our identity as victims. Without forgiving, we become slaves to the offender, who owns our lives. We suffer from offense, while the one who did the damage never gives it another thought, living to spew poison into someone else's life. We render such people ineffective when we forgive them and turn them over to God. Forgiveness is medicine for our healing. We eventually reach a point where we can deflect offense as it is happening to us. It is amazing to have someone looking right at you, intending to deliberately hurt you. You are able to react with peaceful confidence against joyless and unloving behavior. We must forgive to really live.

The next time you are driving in heavy traffic on a two-lane road, be aware of the number of cars coming toward you, all at a high rate of speed. Think about the drivers who are all part and parcel of many national statistics. Assume that each person is battling a problem. Their lives are touched by thoughts of suicide, cancer, death, drugs, alcohol, and abuse. Some are distracted with financial problems or marital problems. Some will experience a heart attack or seizure while driving. Some are rushing to an emergency. Many are angry, speeding or becoming a hazard as they take risks and push their way through traffic to get ahead.

Many of us are severely stressed. We must get out in the flow of traffic every day trying to look and act as if everything is under control and we know where we are going. Maybe the only thing keeping everyone alive as they hurl toward each other is the fact that most people want to keep on living, no matter what their circumstances, crises, or attitudes. Too often there will be someone who does not care and causes a collision. After further investigation, it may be determined there was intent or perhaps just a moment of distraction.

In the same flow of traffic, there are drivers who are peacefully paying attention to the car's performance. They are observing the traffic around them, being courteous, being in the moment, enjoying the morning, and anticipating the day. They left their cares with God in Morning Prayer. They are proceeding to enter the flow of traffic with intent to stay within the rules of the road and make it to their destination. They travel in peace, under control. No matter what happens, they are confident of reaching their destination. They carry equipment and supplies in case there is a need to assist a fellow traveler.

Take away the cars, and we are still in the traffic. Look for the peaceful traveler, and ask him where and how he learned to drive. Ask him what gives him the courage to calmly and joyfully join the flow each day. The answer is the willingness to receive and extend forgiveness and love. If we choose to live in a state of forgiveness and love, the health benefits are endless. They balance us physically, mentally, and emotionally and ripple outward to touch everyone in our path.

There are libraries filled with stories of lives devastated by alcohol, drugs, pornography, and physical, mental, and emotional abuse of every conceivable kind. Unspeakable crimes against others run rampant in the world. Each time we think we have seen the lowest level of humanity; a new and lower form appears. Information assaults our brains during every waking hour, telling us of the world's cruelty, corruption, greed, and insanity, together with random cataclysmic events, all of it coming at us in color, high-def, broadband, and surround sound via at least 250 channels from global satellites. This takes no account of radio and handheld programmable devices. The messages make most of our problems pale by comparison, when we consider our own less dramatic addictions.

The addictions and bad habits of people who fall within the acceptable range of sanity are just as important in God's eyes. He pays attention to every level of separation from him. Popcorn was my drug of choice. Look at your own life, and give the same importance to your individual addiction as the world gives to the obvious ones. It does not matter what the object of desire is; the principles of destruction, surrender, and restoration are the same. We ordinary folks have valid addictions. Perhaps there is no Popcorn-aholics Anonymous national group, but that does not mean it was not a looming problem in my life.

Countless times we have heard, "Look around; there is always someone with worse problems" and "Talk to me after you have walked a mile in his moccasins." They are true statements, but they make us feel that our difficulties are not valid or worthy of mention or repair. Of course we need to act with compassion and understanding for the headliner sins of the world. We also need to extend that same compassion and understanding to other obstacles and transgressions.

When a child comes to a parent with what is a huge problem in his or her world, and that parent dismisses it as nothing in comparison to something "worse," the child is diminished and concludes it's necessary to have larger, more important problems to receive validation. The child will most likely set out to create the kind of crisis that will impress parents. We need to validate every human issue and teach God's way to resolution, through Christ.

Whatever the issue impeding our growth, whether it's critical, chronic, or momentary, God has promised in his word to see us through it. We are important to him. As we move to improve our own lives by extending compassion to others, we learn to express compassion to ourselves. We are valuable to God, no matter what state of brokenness we bring before him. We must have patience with one another and ourselves. We will not always achieve perfection, but we will suffer shorter periods of unforgiveness because we know where to go for help.

Love

The highest and best use, definition, and application of the word *love* belong to God. He is the personification and originator of the word. God's love has substance and meaning. It is unfailing and real when we are walking in step with him in the life he meant us to live. Love is a binding two-way communication of promises and commitment that can never be broken once it is secured through salvation. Before you dedicate your life to God, love is God's promise to you. After you commit your life to him through Christ, love becomes a relationship.

We apply the word *love* to describe our connection to each other. All human relationships are mixed with other impulses and tendencies—sometimes with uncontrolled passion; sometimes with enduring commitment to another's well-being; sometimes with distortion, conflict, and inflicted pain. Many times we enter and maintain relationships to fill our own emptiness or meet shallow, selfish needs. Often the word is watered down to describe a feeling for institutions, abstractions (for example, movies, military history, football), or even inanimate things that can never express love back to us. We become numb to the word. It is used without thought, tossed over a shoulder in our direction. Try to remember the last time you took your angry child's face in both your hands, looked directly into his or her eyes, and said, "I love you more than my own life. You are my child, and nothing you do or say can change my love for you. It is forever." Once we turn our lives over to God and begin to prioritize meaningfully, we realize the sacredness of the word *love*.

One day I was acutely aware that I was making a conscious choice about when, where, and how I used the word love. I realized I was using other descriptive words when referring to material things and experiences. I was reserving *love* for relationships or for a healing word of comfort, support, or growth. We need to develop a reverence for the word *love*, to elevate its use to honor both God and his creations. The giving and receiving of God's love can heal human pain. Living in a state of love does not mean all about us is sweetness and light, that we spit sugar when we speak, or that birds fly above us dropping flower petals before us. It means making love the principle we apply to life. Sometimes it means driving the money changers from the temple. God's love is our core, the well we draw from, and it is always filling us as long as we stay in relationship with God, through Jesus Christ.

Laughter

Laughter is the third component of preventive healthcare. Books have been written in testimony to the connection of laughter and healing. I believe it matters how we laugh and what types of humor we consider acceptable. Humor at other people's expense, cruel humor, gutter humor, and dark, sick humor all reflect the baseness of human nature and have no healing quality.

The humor shared between people with a long history in common is very healing. Distance and time cannot destroy it. It is so finally honed that one word can set off a belly laugh session of loving memories. It is healing to laugh at well-crafted but oddly slanted views of life, the humor that reflects reality. Best of all is the humor generated by children in their newness and by the elderly with their experience as they express their clear, uncomplicated view of the world. Laugh long and hard, until the tears roll, your ribs ache, and you lose your breath. This is healing exercise that will not require a treadmill or stair stepper.

You have to look for healing humor these days. Blatant, in-your-face sexual or sick humor prevails, in an effort to shock, embarrass, and control an audience. This new breed of comedians with their very predictable formula humor only serve to destroy themselves and bore the rest of us. It is a shame because there are some very bright minds out there. They are capable of much better work. They sell their souls for the cheap and easy.

Feed your body and spirit with the love of God. Heal yourself and others forgiving constantly and laughing with joy. The security we know we have in Christ allows us to harness human emotion for our benefit—if we choose to put God's principles into practice and demonstrate them.

I will soon be a Medicare recipient. I have a supplemental medical policy. Should they fail, the basic plan has always been God's original Medical Plan. He put us here for a purpose, and when we have fulfilled it, he will call us home. If we survive whatever befalls us, it will be because God is using our circumstance to show the power of his love. If we don't survive, it is because it is time for us to leave the earth. This very inexpensive policy takes the stress out of living, giving us more energy to put towards living out our brief time on earth with unquestioning faith in our ultimate destiny.

There is no suggestion in the previous paragraph that one should turn down medical assistance if it is available. I am expanding on our ability to be joyful and content as we continue life here in preparation for returning to God. We can experience joy and contentment, even excited anticipation about going home to God.

Life extends beyond this world. There are no boundaries of age as we mortals count them. Our activities here are only a small part of who we are and who we will be forever. These few years, however, are important. Keep in mind, we are all going somewhere for eternity. We can struggle through this world under our own limited power separated from God, continuing the struggle eternally. Or we can live in this world under the direction and care of God and continue in love, peace, and joy eternally. God loves all his creations. He is perfect in love and perfect in justice. We are the ones who make the choice. We do not deserve his grace. We need it. All we have to do is reach for it.

CHAPTER TEN

INTO WHOSE HANDS?

Each of us is the product of generations of choices made by people with whom we share a genetic and familial bond. We know absolutely nothing about most of the past members of our lineage and very little about the two generations behind us, except such facts of their existence as a genealogical search will provide. We are more familiar with our parents, whose power over us we constantly try to escape. Our grandparents, more often than not we know them only at a distance in their elderly state, removed from our world. If we are blessed, they are intricately woven into our lives and represent unconditional love, the mysterious relationship between grandparents and grandchildren. It appears to be born out of the absence of total responsibility for discipline and character shaping on the grandparents' part as well as the absence of the children's need to rebel, which allows them to love unconditionally, often to the dismay of parents.

If we work at establishing and maintaining relationships, we will connect with the one or two generations ahead of us. We will enjoy the few years we will have with the generation or two behind us. Yet we will contribute to the future through our genetics and all of our choices. Anything most of us possess or gather will not greatly influence the future. Our genetic contributions will be diluted and changed over time. The effects of our choices, by contrast, will be felt for generations.

The two foundational choices are these:

One is choosing to be led down the path of human nature, arm in arm with Satan as he feeds our egos, telling us we are self-contained, a god within ourselves, unstoppable and justified in all our human emotions—even though they are controlling us. He will convince us our human nature is the extent of our existence. We had better eat or be eaten. Satan will support us in "doing it our way" all the way down the path. He does not have a written word because he does not need it. Humans are very willing to take the easy road of self; it is their nature.

Satan is the consummate con artist, the originator of lies. He feeds our need to control and makes us believe we control our own destiny. All the time he has us firmly in his grasp. He takes us on, on a case-by-case basis, playing to our individual egos. He looks for a weak moment and steps in to commiserate, to tell us we have a right to "feel" whatever we are feeling and even more of a right to act on it. Satan is all about our individual rights to direct our own destiny.

There is no immutable standard in the world of separation from God. It is all smoke and mirrors. If Satan had written down his word, his eternal plan for souls, it is unlikely anyone reading it would have chosen to follow him. Reward and punishment are one and the same in his world. Satan will walk with us step by step down his path until we are so full of ourselves we do not notice his arm slipping away. The world around us turns to shades of gray. The color and light disappear into a sickening polluted yellow, brown, and black foul-smelling atmosphere. We look ahead into darkness. We look back and see the path is gone. The one who brought us this far has left us to deal with all the consequences of our hedonistic journey. As we turn to view the path ahead, the darkness begins to move toward us slowly.

The temperature and stench increase. We are alone. We have nothing to take with us. We have left nothing of any importance behind us. We have no one at our side. Our future is one of eternal agony and pain of separation from God, forever, because of our own choice. Our choices in life, and the lessons we taught, have left those we claimed to love struggling to make good choices. Some will find their way back to God. Some will follow our example of "self-made" and in turn follow Satan into the emptiness. Never underestimate the influence of our choices. They live on and reach farther into the future than we can imagine.

Have you ever tried to imagine the future of familial ties? Great grandchildren are about as far as any of us can connect with our caring. Yet our choices will live beyond our love. We humans talk about preservation for "future generations," but in reality humans, without God guiding their choices, are not all that interested in much more than fifty years of future. Our choices will bring influence far beyond our moment in time.

Our second choice is to turn our lives over to God our creator, with Jesus Christ our example and the gift of the Holy Spirit as our guide. God's written word and promises are available to all to read, accept, and follow. When we choose to follow Christ, we are loved, protected, and guided on a lighted path. We know Christ will be there for the consequences. Through it all we are firmly locked in an arm that will never slip away, as we press on in absolute faith and trust toward the goal God has set for us. We can never be rejected or turned loose to suffer separation for the consequences of our mistakes. We are connected forever to a love we cannot even fathom on a human level, a love for ourselves and every life. We need only confess our separation, surrender our egos, and accept the love that died for us, a love that forgives everything. Build lives of service as examples of a life in Christ. Then share the story of our surrender and commitment.

We cannot drag, argue with, scream at, physically force, frighten, or guilt-trip people to Christ. We can tell them what Christ has done for us, continue to live the life we have chosen—and love, daily demonstrating joy, love, peace, and service. Then be willing to answer questions when we are asked how we came to this peace. Most renewed Christians are not preachers, teachers, or theologians. We are people who have been tapped for service. We responded to God's call. We witness to others by living a life worthy of the sacrifice made for us.

Into whose hands will we deliver ourselves, our children, and our future family members, by our choices? Do not ever say, "It is too late. I cannot take back or repair the mistakes I have made." It is true we cannot take them back, but we can turn them over to God and let him help us repair the damage. God will instruct us and guide us in the steps we need to take to change the direction of our legacy.

We owe our children more than a callous remark of "Get over it" when they confront us with the pain we have caused them. It will not be easy, because it involves our own transformation, our willingness to apologize, to humble ourselves, going into a free-fall nosedive of admissions of error. We must jettison emotional reactions and personal decisions which have hurt others, ask for their forgiveness, and then trust that, just before we hit the ground, God will reach out his hand and break our fall. We must be willing to lay down our lives to rectify the harm done—leaving loved ones with a clear example of what total commitment (not perfection) can mean in their lives.

We must not follow other Christians into relationship with God. We are to follow Christ. We are responsible for our own relationship with Christ and the sharing of that experience. It is an easy excuse to look at poor examples of Christian behavior among humans and reject Christ. Christians are to band together to help each other progress, not to pull each other down. Committed Christians let no one—friends, fellow Christians, family, foes, or man-made divisions of the body of Christ—ever get in the way of their own relationship with Christ. There are ways, outlined in the Bible, to help others, to keep others from stumbling, and to come alongside those in need without breaking our own commitment. There are steps to take in church discipline, clearly stated in Matthew, to deal with unrepentant Christians in love.

How do we as parents guide our children, using only self as a guide, dragging baggage from a past totally unfamiliar to them, teach them to live in a future world we will know very little about? How do we contribute to the knowledge and skills they will need to cope in a world we are leaving? There is only one way: lead them to God through Jesus Christ. Put them safely in his hands. Step back from the controls, and pray for God's help in guiding them daily. Our knowledge base changes minute by minute. Some of what we know is valuable to pass on. Some of what we have learned is clouded, outdated, and warped by our own earthly experiences. God never changes. God's word is as relevant today as it was when it was written.

The Bible is the manufacturer's instruction manual for life. Parents are not gods. They are taller people who, at best, are two chapters ahead of their children in the *How to Raise Children* book. At worst, they are looking for the library or someone to teach them to read. Many children outgrow their parents at a very early age—especially those cases of arrested parental development. Some children are born with highly developed intellects and gifts. If they are taught to be strong in knowing who they are in Christ, they are able to love their parents for who they are. They do not become stuck where their parents chose to stop. With Christ as their guide, they pass by the blame game and are able to forgive their parents for what their parents cannot give them.

These new soul arrivals to the planet, if they are delivered into the hands of parents who are committed to Christ, flourish through their trials. In the hands of parents who are "good people" who go to church and do the right thing most of the time, they will have to spend more time than necessary finding their way back to God. If born into unfortunate situations, they must begin the struggle to return to God by very difficult trial and error. Too often, instead of being encouraged and led by the authority around them, their innate God-given gifts and desires are ignored. They are discouraged and ridiculed. They are persecuted emotionally and pressured into being carbon copies, forcing them to express their existence in ways that harm themselves and others.

As parents most of us do the best we can with who we are at each moment of parenting. Sadly, most of us parent from the past instead of toward the future. Since no one is born knowing how to parent, does it not make sense to be grateful to God for the solid backing and support he offers? A family solidly based in Christ has the Bible to go to when issues arise. Issues then become the focus. The answers lie in the biblical standards we establish for our families. That helps eliminate the power struggles between parents and children. God's word is the decision maker.

Perhaps we need to change our perception of parenting and view it not as God helping us raise our children but as us helping God raise his children. Then his standards become the guidelines. Conflicts which arise can be answered by the ultimate conflict resolution authority. Children push to gain the upper hand the moment they realize there is not a firm hand in the wheelhouse. They do not want to be in charge. They want to know there are boundaries that provide them security. There is not a single human issue that does not have the solution in God's word. Why would we not want to have full access to his love and guidance? If we destroy, abuse, reject, thwart, or murder these precious gifts of children, we will answer to God, because they are his children.

I did not find my true relationship in Christ until I was in my final glide path, so I could not lead my own child to Christ. I made decisions that had a detrimental effect on her childhood. I sadly had to watch her make choices which impeded her in life. Again, not problems that grab headlines, but relationship and response-to-life problems. We all experience them. We do not have to try to solve them by ourselves. If only we would turn to God through his Son, Jesus, and align our lives with unending love, peace, promise, and protection. Now I watch her finding her strength as she parents her two precious sons into the incredible men they are becoming. I could have strengthened her journey by leading her to a life in Christ. Into whose hands do we deliver the children whom God has entrusted to our care?

It is vital to reach young people with the message that a personal relationship with Jesus Christ will fill all their emptiness. It will strengthen all their weaknesses and reinforce their strengths. His love and forgiveness will give them the confidence to follow those internal callings and fulfill God's plan in their lives. They must be taught that no other human being wants to, needs to, or is able to meet all their needs. We are not required to do that for anyone else. Christ not only can but desires to do so. They must be taught to make Jesus Christ the first love in their lives.

Teaching children about God's sovereignty, authority, and absolute eternal promise is essential for establishing their foundation of core beliefs. They are going to base their life on something. Only one path promises life eternal in love. Children need to know to whom they really belong. Accepting Jesus Christ as the authority in their lives will give them the security, strength, peace, and freedom they crave. Then when they are hit with those stressful, sometimes instant life-altering decisions and situations, they already have a set of solid beliefs upon which to draw. They know who they are in Christ and how to respond.

In order to give children the structure that never changes, we must also believe God is sovereign and surrender our lives to him in example. Children have no respect for authority if that authority sets no boundaries for itself. Children will love us without respecting us, but I believe they would prefer to do both.

CHAPTER ELEVEN

PRAYER, THE ULTIMATE DIRECT SERVICE LINE

What is the first thought in our minds when someone says, "I will pray for you"? Our reaction to that offer speaks volumes about where we are in our walk with God. Do we cringe, snicker, get angry, or write off the person who offered to pray? Or do we feel grateful for the support and consider it a gift of love, believing in the absolute power of the offer, knowing we have a bond with that person in Christ? We are individuals on different levels of growth in our walk with Christ. Christians take comfort in the common lifeline to our Creator. We know the power of prayer is real and necessary in our lives.

Two revelations that came from my transformation have become very important to me daily. One is the certainty that prayer is reverent and worshipful conversation with God. There are times when we engage in formal, corporate prayer. However, the majority of prayer is ongoing communication in our own words: expressing our love and thanks for his constant care, expressing our concern for loved ones, asking what God would have us do in a given situation, acknowledging his beloved Son, and thanking him for all he has given us through his sacrifice.

Knowing about Christ is not the same as knowing Christ. Our relationship with Christ is how we are able to come before God. Christ's death secured our way to God. Prayer is how we talk to our sovereign God through Jesus Christ. There is an order to relationship established by God and explained in simple terms in his word. Trying to force my way to God through my own set of guidelines made life difficult at every turn. When we line up with relationship order, life begins to flow like a river. Yes, there are boulders, snags, and falls. It is so much easier to ride the river over calm water or rapids in the safety of a power boat. Swimming on your own, you are carried into every rock and snag in the river.

My second revelation is that prayer is not one-way. We pray, and then we must listen—listen for instruction and direction from the Holy Spirit, who dwells in us. Our awareness and sensitivity to the answer is all important. The Holy Spirit will signal us when to respond. Then we must move on faith, no matter how it looks or feels. We are here to carry out God's plan.

In my short life as a committed Christian, it has been clear God's directives are seldom easy. The way they point is rarely the way I would have chosen. People who tell me, "God always gives me exactly what I ask for in prayer, just the way I wanted it," are highly suspect as true believers. God does not do our bidding. His will being done means we submit our own will as we ask for guidance and strength to accept and carry out his decision.

When we pray in earnest for a specific outcome, and God does not make it happen according to our request, we humans grow disappointed or discouraged or else find ourselves in a state of fury with God. We apply our "I am good, I go to church every Sunday and have never killed anyone" brand of faith as we pray for someone's life to be spared—and they die. We rail at God, even deny his existence because he did not give us our way.

We must learn to pray for God's will, and for strength to accept God's decision for the person who is ill. Believe God will work in all lives concerned. Know God will be there without fail to see us through the pain or the joy.

Christianity is simple but never easy. The Bible tells us we must be prepared to suffer for our belief in Christ. There is freedom in Christ, and with that freedom comes the privilege of standing up for our belief with total commitment. This sometimes draws friendly fire from family, people we consider friends, and our children—the people who feel threatened by our awakening to a life in Christ. We must stand firm in our conviction about and dedication to God through his Son, Jesus Christ. No one here on earth, no matter how much we love them, is going to assure our eternity. They can never love us more than the God to whom we belong completely.

Moving from Old Testament laws, rules, and rituals, which cannot possibly produce perfection, into the new Covenant is very frightening for people who feel they can control their destiny by their own deeds. To stay in the basics of God's training period, the laws of the Old Testament would place us in the position of limiting God and trying to control life. Abraham obeyed God and left all that he knew to follow God's leading totally on faith. To follow the law, establish a foundation of belief in one sovereign God, and not take the next steps to the freedom though the final sacrifice gives the impression that you do not trust God. God delivered on his Old Testament promise of a final sacrifice. Sin was finally overcome. By accepting that ultimate gift of grace, mercy, and the death and resurrection of Christ, we move into the peace and the eternal light of God's love. This is the promised land he tells us about all through the Old Testament.

The transition from the Old to the New Testament could be compared to learning the discipline and theory of music. You study the basics until you are fully prepared to accept the freedom of choosing the music. Still honoring the foundation of skills and beliefs you acquired from the discipline of your training, you now are free to choose the music. To continue only following the discipline and theory is to stay in the training period. Over time, humans tend to bend, water down, and interpret discipline and theory to create gray areas of obedience. Freedom and trust are frightening. You must give up control, and there are absolutes in a life in Christ. God's word is absolute truth and needs no interpretation by human leaders. His word provides the structure and standards which give us the freedom to concentrate on those things God wants us to accomplish.

Prayer is our intimate communication with God, and the line is never busy. We will never be put on hold. Pray to God to reveal more of himself to you. Pray to understand more of his word and how to apply it to our life. Pray words of praise to God for all he has given us. Thank him constantly for his love and forgiveness. Ask him for direction to do his will and the strength to accept his decision in all things. Pray for the strength to follow his teaching and to withstand the friendly and sometimes the dangerously unfriendly fire you will receive when you choose a life in Christ. Pray for help. Call on him when you are abruptly confronted or attacked for your beliefs, "God, give me the words to answer and act in your name." Pray when the loneliness overtakes you, and it will, because you are separating from the only life you have known when you turn your life over to Christ.

Pray for instruction to serve. Do not concern yourself with "prospering" in a material sense; your needs will be met. There are several definitions of the word *prosper*: to thrive, make steady progress; to favor, render successful; to reach a high point in historical significance or importance; to succeed; to grow, make gain or increase. These definitions appear to make the most sense when referring to the biblical meaning of the word *prosper*.

If you have a problem or crisis of your own, lay it before God. Not for his information. He already knows about it. He wants to know if you recognize what is happening in your life and if you are clear on how to respond to it. Bring it to God, and ask for his answer. Have absolute faith that it will be resolved, and move ahead with what he asked you to do for him. Pray for patience with families and everyone you encounter as you move through this life.

Our prayer life is a way we give back to God the honor, praise, and thanks due him. It is the way in which God feeds our souls and spirits and directs our lives. Once we have accepted the renewing of our soul, and spirit enters in, we are astonished at the intense desire to deepen our prayer life. Pray for the salvation of all people, that they will recognize the call on their lives and choose to surrender.

If we prayed at all in our former lives, we will look back with regret at our pitiful, part-time, halfhearted, routine approach, praying at our convenience, for our own needs. Prayer was very often our last-ditch effort instead of our first-strike defense. Pray for the strength to endure when you have given of your time, energy, and effort in God's work and fellow humans turn on you. Do not be discouraged. We rarely see our kingdom work through to fruition. Were you looking for glory? We are pieces. Our job is to be guided by God to fill our space in the puzzle. To be assured of a permanent position in the whole picture, do everything unto God. The glory belongs to him. Our reward is the privilege and inheritance of eternal relationship with our Father in heaven.

Our most important prayer is the one of surrender with which we begin a real, deep, and lasting relationship with our Creator, our total commitment to true revelation in our lives. We ask Christ to enter our hearts and be the Lord of our lives, to take away the mess that we have made, to resurrect us to be the people he meant us to be. When we accept Christ's loving presence in our very being, we become part of the holy, sovereign Creator's kingdom, forever.

CHAPTER TWELVE

FOR NOW, AND FOREVER

God is perfect in his love and in his justice. He will do what he says he will do, and in his time frame. He has clearly laid out all the guidelines in his written word. There are no gray areas in Christ. Human nature—with its resistance to coming under authority and its self-centered need for shallow emotions—is blind to the strengths of what a life in Christ offers: the everlasting fulfillment of our real needs in a deep and intimate relationship.

Ask yourself if you like the person you have become. Have you been able to fill the empty spaces in your soul with your plan for life? What have you done to make a positive difference in the lives of those you claim to love? If you had to face God in the next five minutes and account for your life, would you meet the requirements for an eternal life with God? Would you be accepted into loving arms, or would you hear the words "Depart from me, I never knew you"? To live joyfully on earth and eternally with God, we must surrender our lives to our Creator and ask his forgiveness. Give him all the baggage and pain we have tried to carry on our own. Choose spiritual life over our shallow, self-involved lives of spiritual death. Then, on being reborn, we must say, "Take the life you gave me, and show me what you want of me in service to you."

God will never give you more than you can handle. That does not just mean burdens. It also means freedom and growth. When you accept, bear, and grow in your faith, he will trust you with more. When you make the commitment to follow Christ completely, God will guide, direct, and allow into your life everything you need to fulfill his plan for you, measured carefully and custom designed for you.

I have finally found a love I can completely trust. It has made relationships here on earth much easier to establish, understand, tolerate, and forgive. When we confront our own human nature we are forgiven and blessed. We are able to let go of lingering anger and frustration with our fellow humans. Not that we won't slip now and then, but there is a way back. We don't have to lose our own lives in anger, blame and unforgiveness.

Christians are commanded to share their stories of God's grace with others. Sometimes we are only sowing seeds, sometimes we are nurturing the seeds, and once in a while we are present or instrumental during the harvest. There are times when we must let others go out of our lives. We learn to bless them on their way. We retain our own peace and pray for God to do a work in them through someone else. As Christians, we know how close we came to missing the gift, and we only want others to know the truth and feel the peaceful freedom of knowing they are loved and secure forever. The alternative to eternal life with God is not something we want even the vilest person to endure. Salvation cannot be forced on anyone; it is a freewill choice. A gift of calling by God.

Living a life that reflects a peace, joy, and confidence others desire in their lives—that is the best evangelizing we can do. God is a loving God. He does love all his children unconditionally, but his care is conditional. His children must choose to surrender to their Creator God. If we choose not to submit to his love and sovereign authority and follow his beloved Son, God will in perfect justice turn each one to his own way of death. I am so grateful for a God who did not give up on me—who kept calling me until I understood and accepted what had always been there for me, what is there for everyone.

How amazing is our Creator? He offers us a totally unbalanced relationship with him. We can trust him absolutely and unfailingly.

He has everything to offer us. We have only our hearts, minds, bodies, and souls to offer him, and even all those are on loan from him. God cannot trust us at all. We fail him constantly. Once we commit ourselves to him, he teaches us about relationship by guiding us through all our slips and falls, always loving us. God gives us many opportunities to dedicate our lives to him and accept our place in his plan by accepting his Son as the Lord of our life. We only need to choose. Time, however, will run out on the offer. Once our time on earth is up, it is too late to make the choice.

God does not expect perfection in us here on earth. He does want us to press on—following his word, constantly choosing to follow the clearly understandable example he sent to live among us. We must turn to God constantly, which simply means turning away from empty flesh-sponsored activities. We must forgive, because we are forgiven. We must love because it is what sustains life. God said it is the most important thing he calls us to do. The flesh, or sin, is just our human nature. Our nature is to choose pleasure for our self-centeredness, following our feelings, wants, and lusts. Without God's protection over our lives, all of us, no matter how "good" we think we are, are capable of depravity on all levels.

Our brains and hearts were designed to be the connections to our Creator. God can work through us to complete his plan for his world. We were not made to stand on our own. We can do nothing of real significance without God. We can barter our souls away to evil and allow our choices to lead us on a path of humanly defined success. Evil will feed your ego and tell you that you are self-made and unstoppable. But God always has the last word.

God gave us the perfect gift of his Son, to show his love for us. He took the gift out of this world through death as we know it—and then returned the gift to show us the power of his sovereignty and his offer of eternal life with him. Then, if that were not enough to convince us, he offered his Holy Spirit to fill us with his peace and understanding, to guide us every minute until he returns for us, if only we will choose life in him though the person of Jesus Christ.

Life on earth, as brief as it is, and life eternal, as long as it is, are too enormously important to be left to human design. We are born for God's purpose. To accomplish that purpose, we must reach our first goal: we must be renewed in spirit. Then we must choose to live in obedience to and reverence for God through the sacrificial gift of His Son, Jesus Christ. When we live in the peace and joy from the indwelling Holy Spirit, we can fulfill God's purpose for us in his world. Be assured of our eternal relationship with him. We really can live in this chaotic, frenzied place in a state of fearlessness, free of worry, full of joy, accomplishing all we were meant to do. We can live a life of peace and contentment, without surrendering our brains. Christianity is not for mindless doormats. Christianity is challenging on a second-by-second basis. I dare you to become a Christian. True Christianity tests our gifts, patience, alertness, loyalty, and integrity. It tests our ability to obey without question and our capacity to love and forgive to the limits.

Following God's plan, knowing without question he is our unfailing support, will give us power to do what he asks of us. Becoming Christians who stay on task keeps us inspired, energized, and occupied. We are persecuted and desirous of more. There will not be enough hours in the day to do all we can in service to him. The passion to grow closer to Jesus Christ does not leave us with enough time or desire to succumb to secular temptations. The things of this world lose their attraction.

We want to respond to the perfect love we are given. We lose the need to fill the emptiness of life with drugs, alcohol, and aberrant sexual experiences or to waste time involving ourselves in destructive relationships or gathering treasures and material possessions. We stop "searching for ourselves" using human values. We begin to love ourselves and care for ourselves by loving and caring for others. God will take care of our needs. We want to stop sucking the life out of other human beings or tearing others down to feel better about ourselves. We stop exalting our own efforts to gain control over temporal things or people. Without God we are nothing, a twinkle of light in forever.

Everything we think we own belonged to someone or something else before we acquired it. It will belong to someone else after we leave. We never own or control anything. Everything can be taken away or given to us in a blink. Without a life in Jesus Christ, we live and die daily by the emotional highs and lows of our human nature. In Christ we can remain peaceful, joyful, and trusting in every circumstance of life. It all depends on your choice. It all belongs to God. No matter how much or how little you are given stewardship of, you will be judged by how you responded to the task.

No one can effectively argue against God. The evidence for God as sovereign Creator and his Son, Jesus, overcoming sin and death is overwhelming, documented, and accepted by diverse peoples worldwide. People everywhere are coming to Christ by the thousands daily. God's truth does not care whether or not you believe in it. His truth exists without your permission or approval. Man's truths change with each person's perception as seen from individual perspectives. God's truth never changes. It is always and forever relevant.

The people who have not accepted Jesus as Lord and Savior do not actually want to debate. They cannot be called to stand for their position, because they cannot document their position. They only have an attack plan. There is only one way to eternal life with our one sovereign God. The rest of the "paths" of all-inclusive tolerance are mere philosophies, created in an attempt to control groups of people and to deify self, and they offer death, not life. Their enlightenments end at the grave. They offer watered-down versions and interpretations of the inerrant word of God. Do not drink the syrupy juice from the paper cup; exchange it for the living water. Many modern-day gurus steal directly from the Bible, spin it in their direction, and sell it to us for $39.95 plus shipping. They give us a financial plan and sometimes even tell us that we are God. They twist God's word to profit from our urge to find answers without having to commit to Christ.

Our human nature wants control, wants to make the rules fit the way we want to live. No human-conceived path to God offers redemption, forgiveness, resurrection, and unending love. No offer of unfailing loyalty. No peace and an eternal life with the Father of our very existence, who desires intimate relationship with his children. No other path offers a living relationship with a sovereign Creator. No self-styled ancient deity, false modern-day prophet, or "play to your audience" preacher can offer us eternal life and completely renew us. God asks that we humble ourselves and accept his gift of grace, follow his word, and live our lives as close to the role model he sent us as we possibly can. Turn to God and choose life, be loved unconditionally, secure and forgiven, knowing finally who you are and where you are going.

The people who believe God believe in his beloved Son, Jesus Christ, as personal Lord and Savior. They believe in his book of loving instruction to us all, and they are gaining momentum. God is calling his people to battle. We have lagged behind in complacency. We have rested in apathetic, infantile Christian attitudes and allowed the enemy to gather strength. God is in control, but he is telling us to grow up in our belief, receive the power he offers, and understand and accept what it takes to follow Christ. Then become a disciple of Christ.

The polarization of good and evil is palpable in the world today. The more we shine light in dark places, challenge the enemy to come forth and openly try to defend his position, the more we demonstrate who God is and how much he loves us. The more we press on, the stronger and more vile the attacks from the enemy will become. Plan on it. The pressure is on to choose to which side you will surrender your life.

Mine has been a long journey, and one of the blessings has been endurance. I no longer regret my lack of world-defined accomplishments or my choices. That would be a waste of the time and energy I have left. Forgiveness is mine through Christ. I wonder daily what task God has for me and how I can be of service. I used to say, "I don't know what God is preparing me for, but I don't think I want it." Now, I can say with all my heart that I still don't know all of what he wants of me beyond this book. Whatever it is, in retrospect, the preparation was worth it. I wait with passionate patience for God to reveal more, in his time, of his plan for the life he gave to me for his purpose.

I am now sixty-eight years new, painfully aware of the many years it took to make that eleven-day trip to the Promised Land. Now that God through Jesus Christ is in charge, I know that all the time I have is all the time I need. When it is time to leave, my eternal peace is solidly assured. This confident comfort is the ultimate gift in life.

As of early March 15, 2009, I was still caring full-time for my ninety-six-year-old mother. I still struggle to become a "daily exercise diva," which has brought me closer to relationship with my physical body. We even like each other now, and I believe we are being prepared for a future assignment. After constantly pursuing answers to my physical problems, because God told me he would help me, I have finally received a diagnosis of spinal stenosis and fibromyalgia. I have been led to information on hormone balancing which I took to my doctor. This appears to answer my weight challenges and many other symptoms which I have had all my life. I have some more testing to go through, but I believe we are finally on the right track. Thank you, God. This area of my life will always require focused vigilance, but the battle for clear answers appears to be over.

My daughter and son-in-law and their sons are moving forward and making major changes in their lives. I look back over my shoulder to keep watch and see them growing and making their choices. I pray daily for them, asking God to watch over them and that they will ask Christ to come into their hearts and lives. I will offer to share what I learn and have learned with family and friends, without fear of rejection, because their choice is truly life or death. God is moving swiftly in their lives also.

It now has been six years since I confronted my husband and my world was shaken to its roots. He has been battling health problems, and they are beginning to win. He is residing in a hospice facility more than a thousand miles away. I had forgiven him. What I had not done was to apply to our situation the act of telling him I had forgiven him. Forgiving is the part that heals us. Stage two is to tell the person, if possible, that we have forgiven them. We need to heal the relationship by talking about what happened to us. We must reach for the depth of pain in the other person and show them forgiveness. Forgiveness does not mean we have forgotten, just that in order to release and move on, we must see the other person through God's eyes and heart, remembering that anyone is capable of all sin, if not for the grace and mercy of God.

One day I was on a short road trip and heard the words in a song to which I had never paid attention. I was overcome with a sense of loss when I thought, "I will never see him alive again." I burst into tears. I realized that time was running out, and a sense of urgency to call him washed over me.

I did love some part of him. I had to tell him he was forgiven and give him an opportunity to talk with me about why he chose to destroy our marriage. I wanted to talk to him about asking God for his forgiveness. I wanted to tell him I had never stopped loving the person I thought I knew. I just could not live with or love what he had done. We began calling each other almost every day. We were able to bring some peace and healing for both of us. Love does not always take an easy course, and we can never see what the people we love see in the people they love. The issue I have to take forward is that, because of my pride, I did not do all I could have done to help my husband.

I loved a man who gave me beautiful letters and cards. He got out of bed at two in the morning to take me out for a ride to overlook the city from across the water. He played beautiful music all the way, just to calm my menopausal brain and stop the flow of tears. He was the man with whom I loved to travel. He ventured off the planned route and did not care if we reached any particular destination at a certain time. He gave words of encouragement and love daily. He supported anything I wanted to do. This was the man who never missed an opportunity to express his love. The one I trusted. Whose company I never tired of, who knew exactly how to make me laugh over frustrating circumstances. The man who made my heart jump every time I saw his face come through the door. That was who I saw and who I missed. Like many of us, he had another side.

My husband died on April 29, 2009, but not before we were able to talk about our relationship. We laughed, cried, and remembered together. We did not want to end in hurt, anger, and unforgiveness. God's love is enough to overcome whatever mess we make of our lives. We all fail to measure up to God's standards when we decide to live without him. The pain comes in having to live with the consequences of our human decisions.

My husband had demons from his past he had never shared with anyone until near the end, when he told me. He did not reveal those things as an excuse for his behavior. He injured the old me. My renewed spirit forgave him. We were both able to move on in peace. We chose to remember the love and strengths of our relationship and forgive the rest.

The issue of my survivor benefits had been in question because of a personnel glitch. It took a new turn with an opportunity to make another plea for my case. I have turned it all over to God's guidance to say or write the words that might bring about a change in the decision makers who handle my case. I follow God's lead. I will accept his decision about the problem. He will resolve it or let me know when to lay it down. There will be no pity party and no screaming victim going over and over the issue endlessly. I am committed to peace in the process and peace in the decision.

There are many more twists and turns to my life not included in this writing. God led me to reveal only those parts of this life that will reach the people he wants to reach. I am growing in Christ, pressing on, and seeking more of God. The excitement of purpose is intoxicating. This is a book about where I have been and who I am at this time of writing. By the time you read it, more knowledge, growth, and commitment will have produced more fruit in my life. We humans are fluid, mercurial. We need to tether ourselves firmly to relationship with Christ and anchor ourselves to God's laws for living.

I know there are those who will tear this book apart and mock its contents with clever sarcasm, just as I would have in the past. It threatens the choice they have made. I know there are those who will respond to the message and begin their own seeking. There will be many people who will fall between those two poles. The words in this book are seeds. They will fall on many kinds of soil, under differing conditions.

Is it frightening to release information like this to the world? Not anymore. Just like all those people before me who have given a public confession of becoming "reborn in spirit," I join the multitudes of truly free people. Free because I am no worse and no better than any other of God's children. Transparency unlocks the prison of arrogance and sets them free to live life in this world, even though they don't belong to it. Free to worship, praise, and love their Creator, humbly surrendering all they are in service to a loving relationship that will never fail. Free never to fear whatever God brings to their lives. Free of dependency on fellow human beings to fill the empty spaces of the heart. Free of the greedy gathering of earthly possessions. Free from condemnation of self or others. Free from self-inflicted emotional pain. Free.

If this book speaks to you, turn to God and thank him for his message. Ask him to forgive your sin of separation. To begin your journey down the rebirth canal, I recommend going headfirst. If this book bothers you, ask God to tell you why. If you become enraged at the message and the author, ask why the message bothers you so intensely. You may be closer than you know to God's call on your life.

We have been admonished in this world not to kill the messenger. We should also be admonished not to deify the messenger. Authors, television talk hosts, commentators, pundits, political figures, celebrities, sports heroes, religious leaders, and many others are only messengers. Listen to their message. What does the message offer? Do the words with which we are bombarded during our waking hours give us peace, joy, love, freedom, trust, and a secure promise of life now and forever? That is what we are offered in a personal relationship with the living Christ: undeserved, unearned love and mercy in God's awesome gift of salvation.

Thank you for taking your time to read and listen to this book. May you seek fellowship with a Christian community of faith-filled fellow human beings who are imperfect in as many ways as they number. They hold the common thread of forgiveness, love, eternal life, and humble surrender to a personal Savior and a loving God. May you come to the full knowledge of Jesus Christ through your own salvation experience.

God loves you, and he is waiting for you. We can reject Christ, but then we can never receive God's gifts of grace, mercy, and salvation on our own. We only need to surrender ourselves, accept and honor the privilege of loving surrender, following, praising, worshiping, and obeying him, now and forever.

Dear heavenly Father,

We all have people in our lives in different stages and ages of life who do not know you. We lift them all up to you. We struggle each day in our own walk to be the people you want us to be. We ache in our hearts for those we know are resisting your gift of everlasting life. We pray earnestly they will seek you and reach for you. We also pray for the strength to accept without guilt the outcome of their decision to receive or not receive you, Lord. We must let them know, as well as ourselves, that Christians are not the saviors. We are the forgiven. Help us demonstrate the peace, love, freedom, and forgiveness a life in Christ offers.

If we truly trust you, God, then we must not chase your children down. We must not use zealous rantings, rigid man-made rules, or guilt and fear in an attempt to drive them to Christ. We are called to spread the knowledge of your love, serving by example and giving testimony to our own salvation. We must do all we can in love to encourage the deep desire in others for their own relationship with Jesus Christ. Help us demonstrate the strength of our commitment to you, by the lives we live. Help us show the people whose lives we touch how powerful the love relationship is you freely offer us and how powerful your judgment is for everyone who chooses to exclude you from their lives.

How grateful we are for the gift of salvation. We pray for the deliverance of those we love. Make us willing to keep walking with you, dear God. Steadfastly letting our loved ones know the most important relationship we have is with you. As much as we love our family members, we cannot go back for them. We can forgive, serve, encourage, and pray for them—invite them to look at all you offer, and then accept the outcome of their choice.

Help us never succumb to loved ones who demand that we choose to love and support them in hopeless, weakened, and temporal relationships or endeavors. For as long as we are able to maintain contact with those we love, we must hold fast to the truth of God's love for all of us and live that truth daily in our interaction with them.

Thank you, God, for your faithfulness, love, grace, and forgiveness. Thank you for the strength you give us to face life. Help us convey your love to those we touch. We pray in the name of your precious Son, our Lord and Savior Jesus Christ.

POST SCRIPT

I am writing this Post Script at the end of October, 2012. Since my mother died on April 9, 2011 I have been in the hospital 7 times. Six of my friends have passed on. We have scattered our parent's ashes, with God's leading, in a perfect way and place. God has guided me through assisting a friend with recovery from a stroke and attendant ongoing health issues.

My grandson nearly lost his leg in a work related accident, and he is beginning his long journey of recovery with God's hand on him and everyone involved. The power of prayer has touched many people through my grandson's experience. God presented me with a situation in a friend's life which was causing tremendous stress and pain. I thought it was beyond my ability to solve. It was, but God said, "Go ahead, I will supply all that you need to finish the job". With God's leading I initiated a law suit, out of state, preparing the documentation for an attorney I had never met. It has been a busy year, but God has been there through it all, giving me energy, peace, and strengthening my faith with every step.

A young neighbor shot himself to death in front of my home. That nightmare served to convince me of the importance of Christians sharing their faith, reaching out to each other to try to make a difference.

God is building confidence in me to share my faith with others when God gives me the opportunity to do so. God has taught me patience, as I waited through delay after delay, for his timing for the publishing of this book.

God has led me to the proper combination of professionals both in the Medical field and the world of alternative medicine producing positive results for the health issues in my body, and so many benefactors who have supported me in my walk. Yes, I now have a program of exercises that meet my needs and I am finally on the road to health. I am growing in my relationship with Christ and wanting more and more of God's word in my life. I am continuing to pare down, sell and give away whatever I do not need. The goal is to live primarily with basic needs, allowing some space for treasures that have been made for or given to me by friends and family. I am being prepared to serve God in whatever way he asks, and I could not be more joyful.

A web site is being developed with the expectation that it will serve to open dialog with others who want to learn to listen for God, share our stories, and pray together, while we move toward a closer or for some a brand new relationship with Christ. I will be learning right along with everyone else.

ABOUT THE AUTHOR

The author is a woman with not one degree or literary credential to her name, she is like you, every lesson learned was "live on stage" education. Like you she was living her life with her own set of ever-changing standards and guidelines dependent upon the situation in front of her. Her upbringing was traditional and secure. Chaos ensued when she went from her home to marriage and life with a fraud. She was alone at age 30 with a child to raise, having had the audacity to file for divorce deep in the territory of a sub-culture who considered women to be property, without rights. Her dreams were put on hold while she struggled to learn a new career, make a home for her daughter, care for ailing parents, battle her own serious health issues with the promise that some day she would take her dreams off the shelf and finish them. She had a major Jesus Complex fed by people around her who came to her for solutions to their problems because she is an effective problem solver. She carried the weight of human train wrecks, allowing them to suck her life away. At fifty-nine she was finally so tired of the terrible load she laid it all down before Christ and said "if there is anything left of me that you can use, it is yours I am tired of the pain of my arrogance." She writes a fast paced, passionate plea for others to examine their lives. Today she lives in peaceful singleness in a remote mountain town in Wyoming, finally beginning to lead the life she envisioned in her youthful dreams. She rents a one room cabin, "Granny's Dorm Room", on the river and is ready to write, blog, interact and learn with other searching souls.